Today I finally got the box open, and I was not at all prepared for what was inside. I never knew what had happened to the girl—it was almost as if she had simply vanished. And then, to find this...

Prudence Willard
May 22, 1861

Secrets of Wayfarers Inn

SECRETS OF WAYFARERS INN

A Place to Belong

BETH ADAMS

CHAPTER ONE

Why do you torture yourself like that?"

Janice Eastman looked up and saw that Tess was standing behind her holding a brown earthenware mug. Tiny wisps of steam curled up over the rim.

"Was I doing it again?"

Tess nodded, and gestured at the jigsaw puzzle Janice was working on. "You know, they make puzzles that show kittens and things. You don't have to do one that makes you sad."

Janice looked down at the puzzle box lid, which showed a beautiful watercolor picture of a seaside, wrapped in climbing roses and flanked by hydrangeas and black-eyed Susans. In the background, colorful sailboats bobbed in the water under a clear blue sky. "This doesn't make me sad. It makes me happy to think of summer."

"That's why you keep sighing?" LuAnn looked up from her book, smiling. She was wrapped up in a soft wool blanket and cradling a cup of tea on the couch with Tom purring beside her. Oh dear. Janice must have sighed pretty loudly if it had distracted LuAnn from her book.

"I guess it does seem pretty far away on a day like today." Janice pointed toward the window, where a sleet-gray sky hung low and heavy. A fire roared in the hearth, the heat was cranked up, and the apartment the friends shared on the top floor of Wayfarers Inn was warm and cozy. But the frigid wind whistled outside, and the temperatures had dropped into the single digits. It wasn't unusual weather for February, but it did make it seem like summer would never come back. Janice slid an edge piece into place and looked up. "Looking at a summer scene reminds me that warmer days are ahead."

"Well, they can't really get colder now, can they?" Tess laughed, then she reached down and picked up a piece of puzzle with a flash of red on it. She held it up to the picture on the box top. It was a part of one of the sails, Janice knew. Beneath the table, Huck, their stray-dog-turned-pet stirred, resettling with his head closer to the baseboard heater.

"Tomorrow is supposed to be the coldest. It should warm up after that." LuAnn readjusted the blanket around herself as an engine revved outside the window. "And at least we're not outside."

"Those poor guys." Tess slipped the piece into the right spot and then walked over to the window and peered out toward the yard, where two men in heavy jackets and hard hats were using a backhoe to dig up the yard. "I can't imagine a worse time of year to be doing that. The ground has to be frozen solid."

"I can imagine a worse time," LuAnn said. "When we have an inn full of guests. Let's be thankful it happened in the slow period."

"I suppose if you have to have your sewer pipe give out, it's better to do it when there aren't many people around," Tess said.

Janice knew she was right, although it was the freezing temperatures that had frozen the pipe that ran under the yard to the city sewer line in the first place. Thankfully, it was only the basement that had been affected, and none of the guest rooms. Their guests, Steve and Beatrice Walton, who were here celebrating their thirtieth anniversary, had been very understanding. But it was still disruptive to have heavy machinery digging outside what was supposed to be a restful retreat at an inn. When Janice looked out earlier, it seemed like the plumbing crew had torn up half the yard trying to get to the burst pipe.

Janice's cell phone buzzed on the counter, and she pushed herself up and retrieved it. *Stacy*. Her daughter didn't often call. She hoped there wasn't something wrong with Larry. Stacy didn't always know what to do when he spiked a fever or developed a rash.

"Hi, Stacy." Janice tried to keep her voice level. Stacy had made it clear that she thought Janice worried too much, so she tried to keep her anxieties to herself. Of course she worried about her only daughter and only grandchild. "How is everything?"

"Hi, Mom. Things are good. How are you?"

Janice heard the theme song to *The Magic School Bus* on the other end of the phone.

"Cold. But aside from that, we're fine." No need to go into the sewer problems right now. "What's going on?" She waited a beat and then added, "Is everything okay with Larry?"

"Larry is fine, Mom." Stacy made a noise that Janice couldn't interpret. "He's been doing great at school. His teacher said he loves playing firefighter at recess and pretends he's trying to save the other students."

Janice chuckled, picturing it. He was such a tenderhearted little boy.

"He's watching some TV."

Before Janice could say anything, Stacy added, "Don't worry. I won't let him watch too much. I just needed something to distract him while I work on some of my online classes."

"I wasn't going to say a thing," Janice said. "You do what you have to do." Truthfully, Janice did think Stacy relied on television to be a babysitter more than she should, but she knew that was typical these days, and Stacy had it tough being a single mom. And Janice's relationship with her daughter could be prickly at times. The last thing Janice wanted to do was upset her over something small.

"Well anyway, I was calling to see if you had any plans tonight."

"Tonight? No, there's nothing on the calendar tonight. Do you need me to babysit?" LuAnn thought Stacy sometimes took advantage of how willing Janice was to watch Larry, but Janice was always glad for an opportunity to spend time with the little guy. And if it helped Stacy out, so much the better. On a cold day like this, they could do movie night and make up a big bowl of popcorn and cuddle under a blanket. She'd been wanting to show Larry *Peter Pan*. It was Stuart's favorite movie when he was this age.

"Actually, no. I wondered if you might want to come over for dinner."

"For dinner?" Janice wasn't sure she'd heard her right.

"Yep. Dinner. That meal after lunch and before bed?" Stacy laughed, but there was something raw in her voice. Something almost vulnerable. What was going on?

"Sure." Janice swallowed. "I'd love to." And then, a moment later, she added, "What can I bring?"

"No need to bring anything," Stacy said. "Just yourself. There's—" Her voice broke off, and Janice's pulse sped up. Was something wrong? Was Stacy sick, and needed to tell her in person?

"There's someone I'd like you to meet."

"Oh." It took a moment for Janice's mouth to catch up with her mind. "A special someone?"

"Yeah," Stacy said. "I guess you could say that. And I thought, well, he's coming over for dinner, and I thought maybe this would be a good time for you to meet him."

"Of course. I would love to."

"Okay. Great. How about six thirty? Would that work?"

"That sounds perfect," Janice said. "I'm looking forward to it."

"See you then." Stacy ended the call, and Janice stood still, looking down at her phone for a moment. A special someone. Janice knew Stacy had been out on dates over the years. It was natural; of course she didn't want to be single forever. But she usually kept that part of her life hidden from Janice. Probably, she had to admit, in part because of the way she had reacted when she'd found out Stacy was pregnant with Larry. If she was honest, Janice could have handled that better. She'd been so shocked, so hurt, so sad for the future she'd imagined for her daughter that had just vanished forever. And then there was the fact that Lawrence had been the pastor of their small church. She'd known it was a stereotype that pastor's kids often got into trouble, but she'd still been floored when it had actually happened in her family.

"Everything okay?" Tess asked. She still stood by the window, her hands wrapped around the mug of tea.

"Stacy just invited me for dinner," she said.

"That sounds like good news," LuAnn said from the couch.

"Yes. I guess it is." She set the phone back down on the counter and plugged it in. "She wants me to meet someone. A guy."

"Well that *is* good news," Tess said. "We'll want a full report."

Janice nodded. It *was* good news—both that Stacy had met someone and that she wanted to introduce him to her. Janice had never even met Larry's father, whose presence in Stacy's life had lasted for only a few weeks, so meeting this man was a step in the right direction. So why did she feel so confused?

She looked up when a loud ringing sound filled the apartment. It took her a moment to realize it was the doorbell they'd installed at the back door, where they received deliveries. She met Tess's and LuAnn's eyes, but both seemed surprised too. They weren't expecting any deliveries today. Winnie, who worked in the café on the first floor, had already gone home, or else she would have been down there to receive the visitor.

"I'll get it." Tess was already walking toward the stairs.

When Tess's footsteps had vanished down the wooden stairs, LuAnn turned to Janice.

"Are you sure you're all right?"

"Yes." Janice sighed and sat back down at the card table. "Just surprised. But I know it's a good thing." She ran her hand through a pile of dark blue puzzle pieces. It was amazing how many different shades of dark blue there were, navy and indigo and midnight blue, and how they all blended together to make it nearly impossible to tell one piece from another.

LuAnn continued to watch her for a minute longer, and then she turned back to her book. Janice continued to sort the pieces, fitting a few into the right spaces in the mass of ocean behind the sailboats. Janice knew she should go downstairs and work on the laundry, or run a duster around the library, or any one of the hundreds of tasks that always needed to be done around the inn, but it was so peaceful in here. Which, she now realized, meant the machines working outside had stopped. Hopefully they'd gotten the patch of yard they needed uncovered and could start to fix the plumbing problem.

Another few moments went by, and both of their cell phones buzzed. Janice went to the counter again and saw a message from Tess.

Come down to the kitchen and check out what they found in the yard.

Janice glanced at LuAnn, who was already pushing herself up. *We'll be right down,* Janice texted back.

"What in the world?" LuAnn asked, but Janice just headed for the stairs. It could be anything. Maybe it was another tunnel, like the one in the basement that had been used to smuggle runaway slaves to freedom. Or maybe it was—ugh, she hoped it wasn't bones or anything horrible like that.

When they got to the kitchen Tess was looking down at something on the table. Two men in work boots and heavy coats stood on the far side. These were the workers the plumber Tom Davis had hired to expose the pipes so he could fix the sewer line. They both looked up as LuAnn and Janice came into the kitchen.

"You poor things. You must be frozen," Janice said, at the same time that LuAnn said, "What is it?"

They all laughed, and one of the men, the taller of the two, said, "We're all right. The cab is heated. But it does feel nice to come in here for a bit."

"We wanted to show you this right away," the shorter, stockier man said, gesturing at what looked like a metal cash box or something similar. Tess had laid newspaper on the table underneath it, and it was about a foot long and maybe eight inches high, and about that wide. Judging by the corrosion of the metal and the rust spots, it had been in the ground for a while.

"This was in the yard?" Janice asked. The sewer line ran away from the river, behind the inn, toward the main line that sat under the street.

"The machine hit it, so we stopped and dug it out," the taller man said. "We didn't find anything else around it, but we'll let you know if we do." It sounded like an exit line, but both men stayed, looking at the box, and Janice realized they were as curious as she was to find out what was inside.

"Thank you," Tess said, lifting up a metal padlock that held the box shut. It was rusted in spots and covered in a layer of dirt. The keyhole at the bottom was caked with grime and moss. "This thing seems solid."

"I don't suppose there was a key buried anywhere near it?" LuAnn asked. Janice knew she was joking, but the taller man responded as if she was serious.

"I'm afraid we didn't find anything."

Janice ran her finger along the top of the box. The metal was cold, and her finger came up caked in grime.

"We could get it open," the stockier workman volunteered. "It would destroy the lock, but it would get you inside."

Janice looked at Tess and then LuAnn and realized right away that they were all on the same page. "Please."

The man went outside and returned a few minutes later with a sledgehammer. "Better stand back," he said, and set the box on the floor. Tess, Janice, and LuAnn all backed up, and he swung the hammer, hitting the lock. Janice flinched, but the lock held, and he swung the hammer again, and once more before the lock gave with a snapping sound.

"There you go." He reached out and pulled the lock off the metal hook it was threaded through. He set it down on the newspaper and hoisted the box onto the table. "Give it a try now."

Tess was the closest, so she reached out and grasped the edge of the metal lid with both hands. She tugged, and Janice held her breath. A part of her was afraid of what they would find, and she prayed it wasn't something scary or gruesome. But mostly, she was intrigued.

Tess had to tug a couple times, but then, with a scrape of metal on metal, the lid lifted on its rusty hinges. The smell of must and something sour was the first thing that hit Janice.

She leaned over so she could see inside. What was—was it possible—

"Oh my," LuAnn said, her eyes wide.

All Janice could do was stare.

CHAPTER TWO

May 17, 1861

Prudence checked her bags again. Had she packed the liniment? The castor oil? Yes, she had. Of course she had. And she had packed her journal and her quill as well. She had everything she needed. The horses nickered softly, stepping in place, while the driver waited patiently on the seat.

"Thee should get on thy way," Jason said. He held Moses in his arms, but the little boy squirmed to be set down. "Thee doesn't want to lose the light."

Prudence knew he was right. She needed to get going if she was going to make it to Anna's home before dark. But it was so hard to leave her husband and young son. Would they be all right here without her?

Patience the goose was squawking about something by the pond, but otherwise the yard was still.

"We will be fine."

Prudence knew that Jason hadn't seen what was in her mind. He simply knew her heart.

"I will care for Moses. Thee does not need to worry about him."

Prudence nodded. Jason loved the child as much as she did. Still, she would worry. She was his mother, after all. She would always worry about her son. But there was another thing she feared. If she wasn't here to meet the visitor who was expected tonight, if something went wrong, it could be disastrous. If they were found out, they could all be in trouble.

"About the package that is set to arrive—"

"I will handle it." Jason's tone was kind, but clear. He had it under control. Nay, she realized. God had it under control. "Anna needs thee now. Go to her."

Prudence nodded, and then, after scooping up her sweet boy for one more hug, she climbed into the waiting brougham.

"We will pray for thee," Jason said. Prudence waved as the driver flicked his crop and the carriage began to roll forward.

They would be fine here. Anna Barton was the one who needed her now.

"What is that?" Tess asked, peering down at the contents of the box on the table.

"Do you think it's okay to touch it?" Janice asked.

Tess nodded, while LuAnn shrugged. Janice wasn't so sure, but she looked around and spotted the yellow rubber gloves Winnie used to wash the dishes. She stepped toward the sink and grabbed them and then held them out. The taller workman laughed, but Tess gamely slipped them on before reaching into the box. The box contained a large piece of fabric tied in a knot, and Tess worked awkwardly in the gloves to untie it. It looked like a tablecloth, Janice realized. She couldn't tell how old it was, but it was a stained off-white color, with what looked like bits of burnt orange and brown. Janice couldn't guess what the original colors had been or how long it had been in the box. She could hear items inside rattling against the bottom and sides of the metal box.

"You want me to cut it?" the taller workman asked.

Janice shook her head, and LuAnn said, "Not yet." They were still on the same page, then. Whatever was in this box, they wanted to keep it intact until they could examine it.

Finally, after what felt like hours but was probably less than two minutes, Tess was able to work the knot carefully out, and she opened the edges of the fabric across the sides of the box.

"What in the world...?" LuAnn walked to the sink and grabbed another pair of gloves from the cabinet underneath, and then she reached into the box and pulled out the top item, which was another piece of fabric, this one in bright pinks and greens. She held it up, and Janice realized what it was.

"It's a dress," Tess said. A sleeveless shift dress in a bright floral pattern. Janice felt a wave of relief wash over her. Whatever this box was, it couldn't be all that old, and it couldn't be as scary as she'd feared.

"It's pretty," Tess said.

"But look at that." LuAnn pointed out a dark brown stain near the hem. It was about three inches long, and it was hard to tell what it was.

"It looks like blood," Tess said, leaning in to get a better look. The wooden table creaked as she rested her weight on it.

Janice knew this was a possibility, but she didn't want to jump to any conclusions. "Maybe," she said. "But it's hard to say. It could be dirt or mold or even something like oil."

LuAnn nodded, though the look on her face said she wasn't convinced. She grasped the tag. "It says Lilly. And then, in smaller writing...Pulitzer?"

"Like the prize?" Tess asked.

LuAnn shrugged.

"Is that the name of the person who owned the dress?" Janice said.

"I don't know." LuAnn looked at it again. "It looks like it's probably the label of the company that made it. But it's hard to say. It kind of looks like the kind of label my mom used to stick in my clothes when I went to summer camp."

"I used to have some labels with my name that I put in all the clothes I made to sell at the church bazaar," Janice said. "Caftans. Nightgowns. That sort of thing."

"Muumuus?" Tess said with a smile.

"They were not muumuus." Janice knew Tess was teasing her, but she still wanted to make her understand. "They were tasteful clothes for relaxing around the house."

"I see." Tess met LuAnn's eye. LuAnn was biting back a smile.

"They always sold quite well too, thank you very much," Janice said.

"I have no doubt," LuAnn said. "And you put your own label in them?"

"So people would know who had made them," Janice said.

"It was sort of like your own clothing line," Tess said.

"Your own line of muumuus," LuAnn said.

Janice laughed. "You'd better watch out, or I'll make muumuus for both of you for Christmas this year."

Tess and LuAnn laughed, and even though she knew they'd been laughing at her, their teasing had cut through the tension that had entered the room with the mention of the possibility of blood.

"So, either the person who made this dress or the person who wore it was named Lilly," LuAnn said, flipping the tag over.

"Or that's the label of the company that made it," Janice said.

"But, look. Someone has written the initials *M.O.* on the back side of the tag."

"M.O.?" Janice repeated.

"So, what is it? M.O. or Lilly?"

"Who knows?" LuAnn said, setting the dress down. "Maybe neither."

"Check this out." Tess reached into the box, still wearing the floppy yellow rubber gloves, and pulled out a tarnished silver bracelet. The metal was thin and delicate, and when Janice leaned in closer, she saw that it was etched with dragonflies, with small blue stones for the eyes.

"It looks like it must have been beautiful once," Tess said, cradling it in her hand. "But the clasp is broken." She pointed to the bent metal pin that should have inserted cleanly into the other end of the circle. She set it down gently next to the dress.

"We're going to get back to work," the taller workman said, gesturing toward the door. Goodness. Janice had almost forgotten they were there.

"Was it the talk of muumuus that did it?" Tess asked.

LuAnn shook her head. "Thank you so much for bringing this in."

"And for your help," Janice added, gesturing at the broken lock. They both turned toward the door, their heavy work boots clomping against the tile floor. A wave of frigid air blew into the kitchen as they stepped out the door. Janice rubbed her hands together to warm them up. Then she reached for a napkin and used it to pull out a crumpled brown sheet of newsprint. She carefully straightened it. A small object fell out of the paper as she lifted it.

"It's a newspaper," Janice said, an idea brewing in her mind. She searched the page and found what she was looking for at the top. It was the *Marietta Times* from June 25, 1964. "You guys. I think this might be a time capsule."

Tess and LuAnn both looked at her, LuAnn's head tilted.

"We buried one at school one time, oh, I don't know, this must have been in the nineties sometime." Janice had taught Home Economics at a high school in Marietta for many years before she'd retired, and she remembered how excited the kids had been to fill the box with items that were meaningful to them. "They put in CDs of their favorite music and a pair of jeans from a brand that was popular and, oh I don't what else. I think there was a copy of the yearbook and the student newspaper in there too." She gestured at the box. "Maybe this is like that."

"Maybe," Tess said. The tone in her voice said she didn't believe it, but she didn't want to say so outright. "Who would have buried a time capsule in the yard?"

"I don't know." Janice shrugged. "Who would have buried any of this in the yard? I'm just saying it's a possibility." She had never said it was anything but an idea. "Anyway, what else is in there?"

LuAnn reached into the box. "I think this is what was wrapped in the newspaper." She pulled out a pocketknife with a tarnished silver handle.

"What in the world?" Tess leaned in to get a closer look. She held out her hand, and LuAnn placed the pocketknife into the rubber glove. Tess pulled the knife open slowly, pulling even as it resisted, but it finally gave, and the blade snapped open.

"Is that...?" Janice couldn't bring herself to finish the question.

"It's hard to say," LuAnn said, leaning in as well. The blade was coated in what looked like a dark brown powder, but Janice supposed it probably hadn't been powder when this box had been buried. It almost looked like it might be—

"It looks like blood," Tess said. "Dried blood."

"Maybe it's rust," Janice volunteered.

There was another pause, and then LuAnn said, "We don't know what it is. We'd have to get someone who knows more about these things to say for sure."

"Do you guys think we should call the police?" Janice asked. "To have them take a look?"

Neither Tess nor LuAnn answered for a moment.

"I'm not sure," Tess finally said. "I mean, if this is blood on the knife, then that opens up a whole lot of questions, most of which I don't really want to consider."

"But if it's not..." LuAnn let her voice trail off.

"Let's see what else is in there before we make any decisions," Tess said.

While Tess continued to look at the knife, LuAnn reached into the box and pulled out a matchbook and a square of paper about the size of a Post-It.

"Dudley's," LuAnn read from the cover of the matchbook.

The name struck something buried deep in Janice's brain. Something she hadn't thought about in many decades. Why did that name ring a bell?

"This says *Corona*." LuAnn was looking down at the paper, where the word was scrawled in blue ink in a messy hand. "Does that make sense to anyone?"

Janice shook her head.

"There's something else in here." Tess had set the knife down and was reaching into the box. She pulled out a bundle of envelopes wrapped in a rubber band. She slipped the rubber band off, opened the top envelope, and pulled out a piece of notepaper.

"'Mom'" Tess read, "'I don't know if you're ever going to get this or not, but I'm writing it because I have to have faith that I'll find a way to get this to you.'"

"Yikes." LuAnn's eyes were wide.

"There's more." Tess squinted at the page, trying to make out the handwriting. "There's something I can't read, and then it says, 'He's been staying out later and later and losing his temper more. He threatened...' something I can't read," Tess said. "Then it goes on, 'I worry he's going to hurt me.'"

"What?" LuAnn said.

"Is there more?" Janice asked.

"It's signed *L*."

"Elle? Like the name?" LuAnn asked.

"*L*, like the letter." Tess shook her head. "That's all I can make out, at least on this one. We'll have to read the others." There looked to be about half-a-dozen letters in the stack.

"Lilly," Janice said quietly.

"Maybe," LuAnn said. "I think it's more likely that's the name of a professional designer, but I guess it's possible."

"Can I see the envelope?" Janice asked. Tess held it out and Janice took it, looking down at the writing on the front. All it said was *Mom*. There was no address, no return information, no postmark.

"L. never sent these letters," Janice said. "Why?"

"And why did they end up in a box along with a bloody knife and a matchbook and a dress?" Tess asked.

"And a newspaper and a scrap of paper and a bracelet and a tablecloth?" LuAnn added.

"And how did any of that end up buried in our backyard?" Janice looked around at her friends, and it was clear that none of them had an answer.

"What do we do with it?" Tess asked. "Do we tell the police?"

"I don't know," LuAnn said. "It doesn't really seem like something they'd want to know about. There isn't really evidence of any kind of crime."

"But what about the blood on the knife? And the dress? And the letter?" Tess was pulling the rubber gloves off, one at a time. "Whoever wrote it thought someone was going to hurt her. Maybe he did, and this is the evidence."

"Or maybe it's nothing dangerous at all," Janice said. She wasn't ruling out a time capsule yet.

"It's really hard to say," LuAnn said. "But I have to admit, I'm curious."

"Me too." A smile spread across Tess's face. "I wonder if we could figure out whose stuff this is."

"And how it ended up in our yard," LuAnn said.

"And whether she's okay," Janice added. "Or even alive."

They were all silent for a minute. The knife, the stain on the dress, the letter saying he was going to hurt her... It painted a sinister picture. Surely after all this time, the girl this dress and bracelet belonged to—L., whoever she was—was not in danger any longer. But what had happened to her? Had she been hurt? Why had someone buried these things? What significance did any of it have?

LuAnn lowered herself into one of the chairs and picked up the matchbook. The background was black, and the word *Dudley's* was written in a blocky red font.

"Dudley's sounds familiar," LuAnn said.

"It's got to be a business," Janice said. "One that gave away matchbooks."

"Not many places still do that," LuAnn said. "But all kinds of businesses used to give them away, back when we were kids. It was seen as good advertising."

Dudley. It wasn't a name you heard very often.

"I know," LuAnn said. "Cynthia. That's why it's familiar."

Both Tess and Janice looked at her. Who was Cynthia?

"Cynthia Cook. She was a guest who stayed here a few months back," LuAnn said. "Back in the fall. I talked with her over breakfast one day. She told me her parents used to own Dudley's."

Janice tried to picture Cynthia Cook. She had a vague recollection of someone with brown hair, but that was all she could come up with.

"It was a tavern." LuAnn turned the matchbook over and over again.

"That's right." Janice sat up straighter in her chair and shook her head. How had she forgotten about that? "That's what it was. It was in one of the old buildings that used to be out behind the inn."

LuAnn was nodding, but Tess cocked her head. "Buildings where now?" she asked.

"There used to be a row of buildings out on that stretch behind the inn," Janice said. "By where the road is. They tore them down, oh, I don't know. Probably thirty years ago at least. They were... Well, back when we were kids, this wasn't the nicest part of town."

"We heard about them at some point when we were buying the inn," LuAnn said. "But there was a lot of information coming at us then, so you might not remember."

"No, I certainly don't," Tess said. "I do remember that this building was used as a warehouse for a while in the sixties. Is that around the right time?"

Janice and LuAnn both nodded. "That's right," Janice said. As hard as it was to imagine, this gorgeous old building that was now decorated with beautiful antiques and nine carefully appointed guest rooms had been used to store grains and fabrics and even tires at one point. It had also stood empty for long stretches, including for many years prior to when the friends had bought it and turned it into Wayfarers Inn. "This wasn't considered a great part of town back then."

Tess shook her head, glancing toward the window over the sink. Tess hadn't grown up here in town, and Janice understood that it was hard to imagine a time when this wasn't valuable real estate.

"This section of town was mainly used for shipping," she said. "And remember, there had been several big floods. It was seen as a liability." Marietta, located at the confluence of the Muskingum and Ohio Rivers, had suffered from flooding throughout its history, including several record-breaking years where water went as high as eight to ten feet within the buildings. There were places in town where you could still see the high water mark from the historic 1937 flood.

"There wasn't much of a tourist industry back then," LuAnn said. LuAnn had only lived in Marietta for a few years as a child, but Janice had always been grateful that she'd met her in kindergarten. "That developed later. When we were kids, no one respectable came over by the river."

"And Dudley's was one of the reasons why," Janice said. "I remember my parents talking about it and hearing about it in church. It was the kind of place they cautioned us against in Sunday school."

"That would have made me all the more curious," Tess said with a smile.

"I suspect some of the stories we heard were overblown," Janice said. "But I wouldn't know." She turned to LuAnn. "And you said Cynthia Cook's parents used to own it?"

"That's what she said. I'm trying to remember exactly what she told me. I asked her what brought her to Marietta, and she said she wanted to see her family's history. She wasn't born yet when her parents lived here." LuAnn's mouth flattened into a line. "It was sad, actually. She told me her older sister, who was just a child, drowned in the river. If I remember right, she said her parents were devastated, and they sold the business and moved and never came back. Cynthia was born a few years later, but of course you never get over that kind of thing, and Marietta remained a place that loomed large in her family's memory." LuAnn paused. "I think that's what she told me, anyway."

"How awful." Janice couldn't imagine anything more painful than losing a child.

"So why would she want to come here?" Tess asked. "It seems like the last place she'd want to visit."

"You'd think so," LuAnn said. "But she told me that both of her parents were gone now, and when she read about the inn, she decided to come see the place that had changed the course of her family's history."

Janice could understand that, in a way, though it still sounded awful.

"When did all this happen?" Tess asked.

"I'm not sure," LuAnn admitted. "If I had to guess, I'd say Cynthia was in her fifties. So if she was born after her parents moved out of Marietta, that must have been in the 1960s or so."

Janice nodded. They couldn't say for sure when the box had been buried, but the newspaper tucked inside it meant that it couldn't have been before June 25, 1964. It was possible the two things were connected, she guessed.

"Do you think Cynthia's parents buried the box?" Janice asked.

"I don't know," LuAnn said. "I mean, I guess it's possible. But it seems like a pretty tenuous connection except for one thing." She reached for the slim silver bracelet that rested on the newspaper. "Cynthia was wearing a necklace with a dragonfly charm when she was here, and I told her I liked it. She mentioned that her sister had been wearing a bracelet with dragonflies on it when she drowned. They never found the bracelet, and her mother always wore the dragonfly necklace as a remembrance." She turned the bracelet over in her hands, looking down at it.

"Do you think there's any way this could be the bracelet?" Tess asked.

"I don't know," LuAnn said. "I mean, it's a pretty strange coincidence if it's not. But I don't know how old her sister was when she...when she passed. This would fit a slim wrist, but it doesn't look like a child's bracelet."

She set the bracelet down on the newspaper, and Janice reached for it and picked it up. She turned it around in her hands. The metal was cold and tarnished to a deep slate gray, but the etching of the dragonflies was still visible.

"Do you think it would be weird to get in touch with Cynthia?" Tess asked. "I'm not exactly sure how you'd phrase that question, but I can't see any other way to find out if this is her sister's bracelet."

"If it is her sister's bracelet, what does all this other stuff mean? What about the letters, and the knife?" LuAnn asked.

Tess shrugged, and Janice shook her head.

"But if it did belong to Cynthia's sister, wouldn't Cynthia want to have it back?" Tess asked.

"That's what I'm trying to weigh. Is it worth potentially bringing a painful subject back up if it's not hers?" LuAnn let out a long breath. "But if it was her sister's, surely she would want it back."

Janice turned the bracelet around slowly, letting her eye trail along the delicately etched dragonflies. The tiny flecks of some blue stone—aquamarine? Blue topaz? —still shone, even covered in layers of grime and dirt. It would be beautiful if it was polished and repaired and cleaned up again.

"I think you should contact her," Tess said. "Worst-case scenario, it's not hers, and we're no closer to knowing how this got here. But if it did belong to her sister, she gets the bracelet back, and we get some answers."

Downstairs, the buzzer for the industrial dryer sounded. The load of towels Tess had run must be done. Janice should really get up and help fold the towels, but she hesitated. There had to be some clue in all this stuff that would help them figure out whose things they were and how they had ended up in their yard. She looked at the items spread out on the table: the dress, the matchbook, the newspaper, the knife, the scrap of paper. What was it that tied all of them together? Whose were they? No answers came to her. She was about to set the bracelet back down on the newspaper when something caught her eye. Was that...?

"What is it?" LuAnn was watching her.

"It almost looks like..." Janice brought the bracelet closer to her face. "I think there's something written here." She tilted the bracelet, and the overhead light caught on a letter engraved on the tarnished inside.

"What does it say?" Tess asked.

Janice squinted. "It looks like numbers. I think that's a nine... Twenty five..." She was pretty sure that was right. "Thirty-six."

"Nine, twenty-five, thirty-six?" LuAnn cocked her head.

"I'm pretty sure." Janice handed the bracelet to LuAnn, who examined it and nodded.

"I think that's right."

"Do you think it's a birthdate?" Janice did some quick math in her head and realized that Cynthia's sister would have to have been significantly older than a child if that was her birthdate.

"It could be anything," Tess said.

"Why don't I see if I can dig up the contact information for Cynthia?" LuAnn pushed herself up.

Tess reached for the stack of letters. "I'll see if there are any other clues in here," she said as she pulled one yellowed sheet of paper from its envelope.

Janice knew that she should probably get up and deal with the laundry or work on billing or invoices. Or she could get started in the kitchen—she couldn't show up to Stacy's tonight empty-handed, and she'd thought maybe she'd make that pavlova Stacy loved so much. It took hours for the meringue to cool completely, so the sooner she got started, the better. But as she started to push herself up, her eyes caught on the pages of yellowed newsprint the knife had been wrapped in. There was a dark brown smudge toward the bottom. It looked almost the same color as the stain on the dress. Janice smoothed the page out. June 25, 1964. Was there some significance to that particular date? The date didn't mean anything to her. Did the newspaper hold a clue, or was it simply used to wrap up the knife? Janice read the headlines: JOHNSON ORDERS 200 MARINES TO JOIN HUNT FOR MISSING CIVIL RIGHTS LEADERS. 7 SOLDIERS KILLED IN PLANE CRASH. RED CHINA BACKS OFF. CIGARETTE INDUSTRY VOWS TO FIGHT REGULATION. The inside of the front page was given over to editorials, one arguing for more oversight of the military and another against a tax hike on corn. Next to that was the last page of the section. The back page was lists of scores for various local sports teams and television listings, and the inside of the page featured the second half of articles that had started earlier in the interior pages. From what she could tell, there was the piece about the missing civil rights workers, who were feared dead, as well as what appeared to be a human-interest piece about an up-and-coming new jockey at the local racetrack, and an article about...

Wait. The article was about the disappearance of Peggy O'Neal. Janice knew that name. It all came flooding back to her. She couldn't have been more than eight when Peggy disappeared, but the kidnapping had sent shock waves through the community.

She remembered her parents sitting her down at the kitchen table and explaining that an older girl had been taken from her bedroom and that they had to be very careful to keep their doors and windows locked. There had been safety meetings at school, and for weeks on end her parents hadn't let her out of their sight. As far as Janice knew, they'd never found out what had happened to Peggy. Was this.... But surely this couldn't be connected, Janice thought.

She read the second half of the article, which must have been published just days after Peggy's disappearance. It lamented the fact that the police had no solid leads on suspects.

"Find something?" Tess asked, looking up from one of the letters.

Janice wasn't sure how to answer. It was only the second half of the article. Surely if someone had wanted to save it, they would have saved the page that contained the first part of the article too. And Peggy O'Neal's name didn't start with an *L*, like the person who had written the letters. But still, the dress and the bracelet made her think this all centered on a girl. Could it possibly be about a girl who had vanished and never been found?

"Maybe," Janice said. "I mean, probably not." She let out a breath. "But I don't know."

A slow smile spread across Tess's face. "What is it?"

Janice sighed. This might be crazy, but she supposed it would be even crazier to not explore this connection. "Have you ever heard of Peggy O'Neal?"

"Nope." Tess tucked her copper-colored hair behind her ear. "Who's that?"

Tess had grown up in a different part of the state, so it wasn't surprising that she hadn't heard of her. It had been big news around here, but maybe it hadn't been a big story nationwide.

"When Peggy O'Neal was seventeen she was kidnapped from her bedroom one night."

"From her bedroom?" Tess's mouth hung open.

"Neighbors saw a car idling nearby, but as far as I know they never found it." Janice tried to remember what other details she'd been told. "I believe there were signs of a scuffle—I think there was a broken mirror and her things were thrown around the room, or something—and she was gone. As far as I know, they never found out what happened to her."

"Oh my goodness."

"Her dad was a bigwig at a bank, from the country club set and all that, and her parents offered a reward for information, but, again, as far as I know, it was never claimed. There was just no trace of her."

"How does that happen?" Tess asked.

"I don't know. It was all a long time ago, so it's possible there were some developments I didn't know about. But I do know that all the parents in town were afraid to let their daughters out alone after that."

"I would imagine the hardware store did a good business in locks as well."

"Oh yes. We checked that the door and windows were locked every night before bed," Janice said. "It was really scary."

"Of course." Tess shuddered. "From her *bedroom*?"

Janice nodded. "It's terrifying, right?"

"It really is." Tess looked down at the letters in her lap. "Could it be connected to this stuff?"

Janice thought for a moment. Could it? But how?

"Margaret." Tess smacked her forehead.

"Margaret?" Janice assumed she meant Margaret Ashworth, the director of the local historical society. "What does she have to do with this?"

"Isn't Peggy a nickname for Margaret?"

"Oh. I guess you're right."

"It has never made sense to me," Tess said. "Maggie or Meg, sure. But Peggy?" She shook her head. "Still. I wonder if Peggy's real name was Margaret."

"And if it was…" Janice reached over and touched the dress. The fabric had a bit of texture and was rough under her fingers.

"The initials make sense," Tess said.

"Margaret O'Neal," Janice said quietly. "It's possible."

There was a pause while they both contemplated this, and then LuAnn appeared in the doorway. "I called the number I had for Cynthia and left a message. We'll see if she calls back."

Janice looked down at the array of objects spread out on the table in front of them. What did any of it mean?

CHAPTER THREE

Janice had just finished making the strawberry sauce that she would spoon over the fruit on the pavlova when LuAnn came into the small top-floor kitchen.

"That looks good." She nodded at the confection.

"Thank you." Judging by the crumbled bits she'd peeled off the baking sheet, the meringue had turned out just right: crispy on the outside, smooth and meltingly soft on the inside. She'd spooned crème fraîche on top and layered it with sliced strawberries. "This was Lawrence's favorite dessert from childhood, and Stacy loves it too."

"It looks quite grand. I'm sure the new beau will be impressed."

"That would be nice, but that's not the goal," Janice said. "I just want to make an effort to show Stacy I'm grateful for the invitation." She pointed at something clutched in LuAnn's hand. "What's that?"

LuAnn sighed and sat down in one of the kitchen chairs. She set the pocketknife, now in a plastic baggie, on the table. "I was looking at this," LuAnn said. "And I noticed that there's an *M* engraved on the handle." She pointed to the tarnished silver of the handle through the clear plastic. Janice leaned in and saw that she was right.

"That's interesting," Janice said. "And the initial M. was in the dress as well."

"M.O." LuAnn nodded. "I wondered if they were connected. But I also wondered something else."

Janice unclipped the blade of the immersion blender she'd used to puree the strawberries and ran it under the faucet.

"What's that?"

"This brown substance that's on the blade. I still think it's blood. I'm wondering if there's some way to find out for sure." LuAnn turned the bag over in her hands.

"I suppose there probably is. Even though it's pretty old, I'm sure there are tests that could be done." Janice set the blender's blade in the dishwasher and closed it. "Are you thinking we should go to the police after all, then?"

"I'm not sure. It would help if we knew whether the substance on the blade was blood or not," LuAnn said. "It's hard to know whether a crime has been committed unless we know that."

"Isn't it?" Janice asked. She'd been mulling this over since they discovered the box. "With that letter saying 'I think he's going to hurt me' and the knife, maybe there's reason enough to show this all to the police. Especially if there's any chance these things are related to the Peggy O'Neal kidnapping." She covered the leftover strawberry puree with plastic wrap and put it in the refrigerator. "I mean, there aren't a lot of reasons I can think of that you would bury all this stuff in the yard unless there was a reason you didn't want it to be found. And there can't be too many good reasons you would do that."

"Maybe," LuAnn said. "I suppose we could start with the police. But I was thinking about Stuart."

"Stuart?" Janice's son was a doctor who maintained a private practice in town and volunteered at a local clinic in his spare time. Janice was extremely proud of him, but she didn't see what he had to do with any of this. "What do you mean? I don't think his office has the facilities to test something like this."

"No, I wasn't thinking of his office," LuAnn said. "I mean, there's probably some lab he could send it out to, but that's not what I had in mind."

Janice wiped her hands on the dishrag, waiting for LuAnn to go on.

"He's the town coroner, right?"

"Yes," Janice said. She saw where LuAnn was going now. In addition to his medical practice, Stuart served as the coroner for Marietta when the need arose. "That's an interesting point."

"Do you think he would have access to the equipment to test the substance there?"

"I don't know," Janice said. "I've never asked him too much about that aspect of his job." It had always seemed quite morbid, honestly, and she didn't really want to know all the details. "I suppose I could ask, if the police aren't interested."

LuAnn nodded. "Why don't I give Chief Mayfield a call? We'll see what he says and take it from there."

"That sounds good." Janice looked at the pavlova resting on the portable dessert tray that had served her well through so many church potlucks. The confection glistened with ripe fruit piled on creamy filling and crispy meringue. It looked good, if she did say so herself. LuAnn followed her glance.

"You have to bring home any leftovers," she said with a smile.

"I'll do my best," Janice said, though she was pretty sure there wouldn't be too much left over. "Now I should get going if I'm going to make it to Stacy's by six thirty." She lifted the apron over her head and hung it on its hook by the door.

"Tell her we say hi," LuAnn said. "And give Larry a hug for me."

"I will." Janice ducked into her bedroom and changed into pressed slacks and a wool sweater in a soft coral color. Then she gathered up the toy cars she'd picked up for Larry in the checkout line the last time she'd been at the store—she couldn't help buying little treats for him—and tucked them into her purse. Then she waved goodbye to LuAnn and Tess, who had come up from the basement, grabbed the dessert carrier, and took the elevator down to the first floor. A bitter wind whipped off the river and blasted her as she stepped outside, and she pulled her scarf up over her nose and hurried out to her car. Night had already fallen, and the workers were done in the yard, but the backhoe still sat in the grass, and the ground was torn up in a wide line from the basement to the street that ran behind the inn. She sure hoped they'd be able to get that looking presentable again soon. It didn't do much for the inn's image.

Stacy lived on the far side of town, in a small house near a park. Janice had lived in an apartment over the garage before she had moved to the inn. Janice looked forward to seeing Stacy and Larry, but tonight she felt strangely nervous. Stacy had met someone, and Janice wasn't sure what to expect.

For so many years, starting when Stacy was just a girl, Janice and Lawrence had prayed for God to bring a strong Christian man into their daughter's life, but Stacy had never seemed to be interested in any of the eligible men at church. Frankly, she hadn't been interested in much about church at all, and as far as Janice knew, she hadn't attended in years. Stacy didn't share much about her spiritual life with Janice, and Janice had slowly come to accept that her role for the time being was to pray that Stacy would know how much God loved her, no matter what. Still, she couldn't help but hope that the man Stacy wanted her to meet would draw her daughter closer to the Lord.

Janice clung to the handrail and tucked her head against the wind as she climbed the cement steps that led to Stacy's front door. Someone had sprinkled rock salt on the steps in anticipation of a snow shower that was supposed to blow through tonight, and it crunched beneath her feet as she made her way toward the door. She balanced the dessert tray and her purse on one arm and rang the doorbell, and a few moments later, the door opened.

"Hi, Mom." Stacy's cheeks were flushed, and her curly brown hair was pulled into a messy bun. Something was different about her.

"Hi there." Janice studied her daughter, trying to figure out what had changed. She wore a tight black T-shirt and jeans, but that was her typical uniform. She wore just a hint of mascara and some lip gloss, but then she'd been wearing far less makeup ever since Larry had been born, so that wasn't unusual either. "It's so good to see you. Thank you for having me over."

"Come in. That looks wonderful." Stacy took the dessert tray out of her hands. "You didn't have to do that, Mom. I made brownies." She gestured to a pan cooling on the counter.

Oh. Brownies. "I know how much you love pavlova, and I wanted to do something special." Would Stacy *rather* have brownies? Was she upset that Janice had brought dessert? Janice tried to read her face. She had wanted to do something nice, but had she overstepped? She never seemed to know what would upset Stacy.

"It looks great. Thank you." Stacy smiled, and it seemed to Janice that it was genuine, and she felt a tiny bit better. "I appreciate that you made it," Stacy added almost as an afterthought, and Janice realized that Stacy was nervous. She was trying hard to make this evening go well, and Janice felt a surge of affection for her daughter.

She set her purse by the door and looked around. Usually there were toys strewn around the small living room, but it looked like Stacy had picked them up. "Where's Larry?"

"Dash is reading him a story. Hang on."

Dash? Surely she hadn't heard that right. What kind of name was Dash?

Stacy ducked down the hallway and called, "Larry, Nana is here."

There was a squeal, and a moment later, her towheaded grandson came running down the hall. "Nana!" He flew into her arms, and she wrapped him a hug. She would never get tired of this, she thought as she pulled him tighter.

She'd been so upset when she found out Stacy was pregnant, so convinced her daughter had ruined her future, that she'd been completely unprepared for how gobsmacked she'd been when she held her grandson for the first time. Holding baby Larry was not at all like holding her own children, she'd quickly come to understand. She had loved him with a deep, abiding, unquestioning love, distinct from and yet wrapped up in the fierce protective love she'd felt as a mother. Sure, the circumstances of Larry's birth were not what Janice would have chosen for Stacy, but little Larry made her forget all that the moment she held him.

"How are you?" She set him down and saw that he'd grown since she'd seen him last, and he'd had a haircut. He was looking more and more like Lawrence every day, with his grandfather's big brown eyes.

"Good. We saw a car carrier on the way home today."

"Oh my goodness. That's exciting." Larry was obsessed with vehicles of all kinds.

"It had six cars on it," he added, smiling.

"That is a good day, then." She pulled the cars from her purse and held them out. "Did any of them look like these?"

Larry whooped as he saw the small metal cars. "Awesome. A Stingray!" He pulled out a silver car with red and blue stars on it. "And a Viper!" This car was light blue and had a tail on the rear.

Janice laughed. "Is that what they are?"

"Thank you, Nana." He took the cars and ran down the hall toward his bedroom, where Janice knew he would add them to his ever-growing collection.

Stacy cleared her throat as Larry vanished down the hall. Janice saw a man standing in the doorway. "Mom, I'd like you to meet Dash. Dash, this is my mom."

Dash stepped forward and held out his hand. He was tall and burly, with a thick brown beard and dark eyes. But what were those things in his ears? There were holes in his earlobes, held open by what looked like some kind of earring.

"It's great to meet you, Mrs. Eastman." His voice was deep, with a bit of a northern accent. The sleeves of his flannel shirt were rolled up, and she saw tattoos snaking up his forearm.

"It's nice to meet you too," she said, trying to keep her voice level.

"Stacy has told me so much about you," he said, maintaining a smile. Janice couldn't say the same, so she nodded.

"The inn you run sounds really wonderful. Stacy said there are real Underground Railroad tunnels in the basement," he said.

"That's right," she said, trying to force her face into a smile. "My friends and I opened it a little over a year and a half ago, and we really love it, even though it's a lot of work."

"I can imagine." He turned as Stacy handed him a stack of plates, and he started to set them around the table.

A rush of warm air erupted from the oven when Stacy opened the door.

"And what do you do for a living?" Janice asked.

"I'm an artist," he said as he set a plate down at the head of the table.

"Oh," she said, and then struggled to figure out what else to say. Of course. Stacy never had been one to go for the lawyers or the accountants, or anyone with a steady paycheck. Still, she couldn't be too quick to judge. There were all kinds of art, and she was sure some artists could have stable careers. Janice tried to keep her voice level as she said, "That's interesting."

Stacy hit the oven door a little harder than necessary, and it banged as it shut.

"What is your medium?" Janice asked.

"Mixed media, for the most part." Dash set the last plate down on the table and turned to grab a stack of napkins from the dispenser on the counter.

"Mixed media?" Janice repeated, trying to make sense of the words. "What is that?"

"I use a number of different materials, but all found objects, in one piece," he explained as he set a napkin alongside each plate.

Janice nodded. "Found objects" sure made it sound like he collected junk and stuck it on his pictures, but she knew better than to say that. "It sounds like collage."

Dash paused a moment before he said, "Yes, I guess you could say that."

"That's interesting," Janice said.

Was she imagining it, or did Stacy bang the lasagna tray down on the counter a bit harder than was necessary?

"Right now I'm working on a piece about climate change, using lots of plants to open up conversation about the way growing patterns are changing."

"Oh." Janice didn't know what to say, so she repeated, "That is very interesting."

Dash nodded as he stepped into the kitchen and opened the silverware drawer.

"Mom, can you bring the salad to the table?" There was an edge in Stacy's voice, one Janice couldn't pinpoint. What was eating her?

"Of course," she said, stepping past Dash to grab the glass salad bowl from the counter. "This looks good." The salad was made with some kind of delicate greens she couldn't identify, topped with apple and pistachios and crumbled blue cheese.

"Dash works part-time down at the co-op," Stacy said, "and he gets a great deal on produce."

"That's nice." Janice knew about the organic food co-op over on the outskirts of town, but she had never been inside. She had the impression they mostly sold overpriced vegetables and bulk bins of cereals made out of hemp. You had to bring your own tote bags, and there were bins outside where you could recycle textiles. "I've been meaning to check that place out."

If she didn't know better, she could have sworn she heard Stacy snort.

"Do you like it there?" Janice continued.

"Oh yeah. It's great. All the meat is hormone- and RBST-free, and it's grass-fed, so you can feel good about it. That's important to me." Dash smiled. "You should check it out. I'll give you a tour."

"That sounds interesting." Janice set the salad on the table. No matter how she felt about the co-op, the fact that he worked there meant that he apparently wasn't making enough at his art to live on. Not that that was a huge surprise, really, with collages.

"Here's the dressing," Stacy said, her voice overly cheerful. She set cruets of olive oil and what looked like balsamic vinegar on the table.

"Yum," Janice said, keeping the smile pasted on her face. "And how did you two meet?"

"Online," Dash said.

"Oh." Online. Janice knew that lots of people met online these days, and that many of them went on to have very successful relationships. But what did you really know about someone when you met them over the internet? It wasn't like when you met someone in real life, at school or church. You could be anyone on the internet, that's what everyone said. But still, she kept the smile on her face. "How interesting."

Stacy came up behind her holding a basket of garlic bread. "Dash, do you mind getting Larry?" she asked.

"Sure thing." Dash ducked down the hallway, almost like he couldn't wait to get away. As soon as he was out of earshot Stacy set the pan down on the table and turned to face her. "Mom, do you have to be like this?"

"Like what?" What was she talking about?

"You didn't even give him a chance. You just came in here and started making assumptions, and it's not fair. He's a really nice guy, and—"

"What did I do?" Janice was baffled. She thought she'd been doing a fine job of being pleasant, especially given the situation.

"You've said 'that's interesting' about five times. Which is what you say when you're judging something."

"I do not—"

"I like him, and I was hoping you would be able to see past the tattoos and spacers and see how great he is, but I guess I should have known better."

Spacers? What were spacers? But Janice didn't need to get distracted. "It's not that I don't like him," she said.

"Then what?" Stacy asked.

Janice felt herself shrink. She pressed her lips together and took a moment to compose her words. But Stacy jumped into the silence and said, "Larry adores him."

"That's part of what I'm worried about," Janice said. "You need to be careful. You've got a little boy to consider, and you can't jump into things and let him get attached when—"

"Let's not talk about it," Stacy said as Dash's footsteps came back down the hallway.

Janice looked up and saw that Dash had Larry draped over his shoulder, Larry's little legs flailing behind him. He was laughing, pretending to pound at Dash with his fists. Janice sucked in a breath as Dash swung him around and set him on the ground.

Larry did seem to like him. But what happened if they broke up? Larry would be devastated.

Janice gave Stacy a smile, but Stacy didn't meet her eyes as she gestured for Larry to sit at the table. Janice settled herself in across from Dash. Stacy had always preferred to live for the moment instead of thinking about the long-term consequences of her actions. She needed someone stable in her life, someone who could protect her from herself in so many ways.

"Shall we eat?" Stacy said with forced cheerfulness.

"This looks great," Dash said.

"It sure does." Janice put the napkin in her lap and smoothed it out.

"I want cereal." Larry's bottom lip stuck out.

"We're having lasagna," Stacy said.

"Is it spicy?" Larry asked.

"No, it's not spicy," she replied. "It's got that sausage you like." Stacy turned to face Janice. "Now, how big of a piece should I cut you, Mom?"

Suddenly, she wasn't all that hungry, but she told Stacy to cut her a nice big piece anyway, and then Stacy served the others.

"Dig in." Stacy set down the knife and picked up her fork.

Normally Janice would suggest that they pray first, but she didn't dare. Instead, she looked down at her plate, unsettled and uncertain.

CHAPTER FOUR

When Janice came into the living room Friday morning, Huck and Tom were both crouched over their food dishes and LuAnn was sitting at the table, flipping through what looked like a dictionary. There was a stack of other thick books and a mug of coffee sitting next to her, and she seemed to be muttering to herself.

"Good morning." Janice pulled the belt of her robe tighter against the morning chill.

LuAnn looked up and smiled. "Well, hello there. Did you sleep all right?"

Truthfully, she'd tossed and turned the whole night, replaying the evening with Stacy over and over in her head, trying to figure out where it had all gone wrong. Had she done something wrong? It seemed like Stacy was always ready to be offended by what Janice did and said. But she couldn't go into all that now. Not before coffee. "Just fine."

"There's coffee on." LuAnn pointed to the pot on the counter.

"Bless you." Janice poured herself a cup of rich, steaming coffee and added milk and sugar, and then she wandered over to see what LuAnn was working on. "Some light reading?"

LuAnn took a sip and laughed. "More like exercise. I got a workout digging all these out." She gestured toward the stack of books.

"What is all this?" Janice sat down and picked up the top book in the stack. She saw that it was a Spanish-English dictionary.

"My collection of reference books."

Underneath the Spanish book was a thesaurus, a book of world history, and a book written in a language she didn't understand, as well as several others she couldn't identify.

"Okay." Janice took a sip of the coffee. It was warm and delicious. "I suppose I need to ask the obvious question. Why?"

"Well, I started the morning by reading through the letters that were in the box."

"The ones signed by L.?"

LuAnn nodded. "It's pretty much like Tess said after she read them yesterday. They're clearly written by a girl who misses her mom. But she doesn't seem to know where her mom is or whether she'll ever get these letters."

"That sounds sad."

"It really is. She lives with some man—maybe a dad, maybe not—and he's hard on her. He seems to drink too much and get violent. Sounds like a real doozy. And there are some references to a person named R."

"Is there anything at all that would give us a clue about who she is?"

"Not that I saw." LuAnn pointed to the stack of books. "So to cheer myself up, I turned to linguistics."

"You and I have very different ideas of a good time."

"No doubt." LuAnn pointed to the open book in front of her. "I'm trying to make sense of the word *corona*."

"Ah." Janice saw now. The word that had been written on the paper in the box they'd uncovered the day before. In the midst of the mess with Stacy, Janice had almost forgotten about that. "What are you finding?"

"Not much that's useful." LuAnn looked down at an open notebook in front of her. "It means 'crown' in Latin and Spanish."

"So maybe it's a reference to royalty," Janice suggested.

"Maybe." But LuAnn seemed dubious. "It's the name of a neighborhood in Queens, New York. So maybe there's a connection to New York City somehow. It's also the name of a brand of beer. Which makes sense if there's a connection to the tavern Dudley's." She shrugged. "It's also a type of cigar, and it's the name of the outer layer of the sun's atmosphere, that part that glows around the edges like a halo."

"Huh." Janice had never known that was what it was called. "So do we think whoever buried the box worked for NASA?"

"Unlikely. It also doesn't seem likely that we're dealing with a cigar aficionado, though I suppose you never know."

Janice took another sip of the coffee and wrapped her hands around the mug. "So basically you're saying you can't make heads or tails of it."

"That's about right." LuAnn stretched her arms over her head and let out a sigh. "It was worth a try, though."

"I'm impressed. I didn't even know you had all these books in your room."

LuAnn gave her a crooked smile. "Old habits die hard."

LuAnn had taught English and history at a high school in West Virginia before she'd retired and moved to Marietta. Janice supposed the books made sense after all.

LuAnn started to push herself up. "I need to go downstairs and help Winnie get breakfast started," she said. "But so you're aware, Randy Lewis came by to take a look at the box and its contents last night."

"What did he say?" Randy had been in Janice's Sunday school class two decades ago, and she still thought of him as the hyperactive little boy with a gap between his two front teeth.

"He couldn't tell if the brown substance on the knife and the dress was blood or not by looking at it, but he did take the knife to check it out." LuAnn closed the dictionary in front of her and sighed. "It doesn't mean I'm going to stop trying to figure out what happened in the meantime though."

"Of course not." Janice drained the last of the coffee from her mug.

LuAnn laughed, a soft, resigned laugh. "If only I knew where to start." She carried her mug into the kitchen and set it into the dishwasher.

Janice walked over to the window and pulled the curtain back. A dusting of snow had fallen overnight, and the yard was covered with a fine layer of white powder.

"What about the dress?" she said.

"What about it?" LuAnn turned, leaning against the counter.

"Randy took the knife, so Stuart can't test that to see if the dark stain really is blood. But what about the stain on the dress?"

"Do you think he would be able to test the fabric?" LuAnn asked. "How does that work?"

"I don't know," Janice said. But her mind was whirling, thinking through the possibilities. Was there any way... Surely it wouldn't work....

"What are you thinking? You have an idea, I can see it."

Janice ran through the idea in her mind. She knew it worked on fresh blood, but would it work on blood over fifty years old? And what if it wasn't blood after all?

"I don't know if it will work," she finally said.

"If *what* will work?"

Janice thought about it for a minute longer, though she could see that LuAnn grew more frustrated with each passing moment. Finally, she said, "Hydrogen peroxide."

"What?"

"Hydrogen peroxide gets blood stains out of fabric." So many people thought Home Ec was less important than Coding and Mandarin and whatever else kids were learning in schools these days, but Janice found that she was constantly using knowledge she'd squirreled away over the years. "When you pour hydrogen peroxide on a blood stain, it reacts to the blood and bubbles."

"Just like it does on a cut?"

"Exactly. And when it's poured on a dried blood stain, the bubbles lift the stain away."

"I see," LuAnn said. "So you think that if we pour hydrogen peroxide on the dark spot on the dress and there is a reaction, then it's blood."

"I can't say for sure. Even if it really is blood, I don't know if it will work on a stain that's decades old. But I think it would be worth trying." Janice didn't understand how it worked exactly. It was some kind of chemical reaction between the peroxide and one of the compounds in blood, she thought. All she knew was that it usually lifted a blood stain right away. She'd saved more clothes this way through the years.

"I agree," LuAnn said. She looked at the clock over the sink. "Winnie can get breakfast started, and I'll join her in a few minutes."

"There are only two guests here," Janice said. There were supposed to be two more guests checking in today, but there was plenty of time to prepare for their arrival. "I'm sure Winnie can handle getting breakfast started for them and then we'll help her get ready for the café to open."

LuAnn went to get the dress from the box, which was sitting next to the couch, while Janice went into her bathroom and took the bottle of hydrogen peroxide from the medicine cabinet as well as a few cotton balls.

"We probably want to test just a small section," Janice said as LuAnn spread the dress out so the stained section was showing. The pink and green pattern was especially bright against the gray morning light. "That way there's plenty left to test in more official capacities."

"I don't see what could be more official than this," LuAnn said, laughing. "Two middle-aged innkeepers using first aid products in their kitchen? Sounds official to me."

Janice laughed as she opened the bottle and turned it over to wet a cotton ball. Then she reached out and gently rubbed a small section of the brown stain. She realized she was holding her breath, but she let it out when the stain started to bubble and foam.

"So that's blood," LuAnn said.

"It seems likely it is," Janice said.

"I don't know whether to be glad or not," LuAnn said. "I like being right. But I don't love what this probably means."

Janice watched as the blood continued to foam and then slowly fizzle out. How had a dress stained with blood ended up in their yard? How had the blood gotten onto the dress in the first place?

"It's probably fair to assume that it's blood on the knife too, then," LuAnn said.

"Probably," Janice said. That was the logical conclusion, of course. Someone had probably been stabbed or cut with the knife. But was it the person wearing the dress? Or had the dress just been tossed into the box with the knife, and if so, why? "Though I suspect the police might do some more official tests to decide that."

"Luckily for us, we don't need to waste time wondering," LuAnn said.

Janice nodded, thinking. "It might help, though. To do some more tests, I mean." Would Stuart be able to tell them anything more? "They might be able to find some DNA in the stain, which could help us identify whose blood it is."

LuAnn folded the dress. "Are there any Home Ec tips for how to use everyday products to test for DNA?"

Janice laughed. "Sadly, not that I'm aware of." She tossed the cotton ball in the trash. "But Stuart might be able to."

"All right then," LuAnn said. "How quickly can you get it to him?"

"I'll take it over to his office this morning," Janice said.

"That sounds like a plan." LuAnn turned toward the stairs. "I suppose I should go down and help Winnie."

"And I should probably get dressed."

"I don't know. What could be more official than a bathrobe?"

LuAnn chuckled to herself as she headed down the stairs, and Janice poured another cup of coffee. She wandered over to the card table where the jigsaw puzzle was set up and slid a few pieces into place while she sipped. The picture was coming together slowly, one fragment at a time. She just had to keep fitting the individual pieces into place and the whole picture would become clear.

Tess was stirring in her room by the time Janice was done with her coffee, and Janice headed into her own room to get dressed and ready for the day. But she was no closer to fitting together the pieces of the puzzle about how the box ended up buried in their yard.

CHAPTER FIVE

When Janice arrived at Stuart's office, there was already a handful of people in the waiting room. A tired mother with a listless toddler sprawled in her lap smiled as she came in, and a woman with curly gray hair and support hose looked up from her magazine as Janice walked toward the reception counter.

"Hi, Bailey," Janice said, and the young woman behind the desk looked up as she approached.

"Hi there, Mrs. Eastman." Bailey was in her midtwenties and had wheat-colored hair and a ready smile. Stuart had hired Bailey to give Stacy, who still worked here part-time, more time for her schoolwork. Bailey now handled most of the billing and insurance issues for the office, but she also did a great job of making everyone who came into the office feel welcome. "It's good to see you. Oh no. Did you get that flu that's going around?"

"No, thankfully not," Janice said. "I was actually just wanting to talk to Stuart."

"Oh good." Bailey smiled. "Is he expecting you?"

"No. I was hoping to grab a minute or two to speak with him between appointments."

"All right then. Go ahead and have a seat, and I'll let him know you're here." She gestured toward the waiting room.

"Thank you." Janice turned and took a seat on the chair in the corner. She'd helped Stuart pick out the decor and furnishings for the office, and she was glad she'd convinced him to go for the upholstered chairs. He'd been worried that they would stain easily, but Janice thought the blue and gold pattern contrasted nicely with the honey wood and the warm beige on the walls, and the watercolors gave the whole room a welcoming, homey feel.

Janice pulled a book out of her purse and tried to read, but her mind kept drifting back to the dress, the knife, and Peggy O'Neal. She was glad when a mother and teenage girl came out from the back and Bailey indicated that she should head into Stuart's office. Janice walked down the hallway past several examination rooms to the open door at the end of the hallway.

Stuart was seated behind a desk and looked up from a computer screen as Janice walked in.

"Hi, Ma." He finished typing something and then turned to her. Janice sat down and hoisted the tote bag she'd used to carry the dress into her lap. There was a framed picture of Zelda, Stuart's fiancé, on his desk. Janice's first instinct was to ask if he and Zelda had set a wedding date yet, but she bit her tongue. Apparently she'd asked that enough in the past few months that Stuart had gotten fed up and promised to let her know when they had it nailed down. Between Zelda's touring schedule, her daughter Brin's school calendar, and Stuart's own multiple jobs, it was harder than they'd expected to find a date that worked. "What's going on?"

"Hi, Stuart. Thank you for making the time to talk with me. I'll be quick because I know you've got a waiting room full of patients."

"Of course." He nodded, and his brown hair flopped in front of his eyes. He brushed it back absently. He needed a haircut, but Janice didn't say so. "I assumed it must be pretty important."

"It is," Janice said, but her voice faltered a little. Was this fifty-year-old dress more important than that little boy with a fever in the waiting room? But Janice plowed on. "I was wondering if you could help me with something."

She had wrapped the dress in tissue paper and sealed it inside an extra-large freezer bag, and she pulled it out now and unfolded it gently.

"I'm hoping you could help me make sense of this stain," she said, pointing to the brownish splotch on the front. "I'm pretty sure it's blood, but I'd love to know if there's any DNA or anything like that that you could find."

"What is this?"

He looked worried, and Janice realized that without context, this must be kind of a strange question.

"Don't worry," she said, and quickly filled him in on the box and the questions it raised. "We're hoping this might be the key to an unsolved crime. But it's from decades ago if it is."

"If that's the case, the police need to be testing this stain, not me," Stuart said. When he wrinkled his brow like that, he looked so much like Janice's father.

"The police took the knife to test," Janice said. "But they left this. And I used hydrogen peroxide to test the stain, and it bubbled, which means it's blood. So I'm hoping to find out whose blood, or anything else you can tell me. Is that something you can test?"

Stuart took in a deep breath and let it out slowly. "It depends. If the stain is very old, there's a good chance the genetic material has degraded over time. But if it's been in a sealed airtight box, away from heat and sunlight, we might get lucky." His computer dinged, and he looked over at it briefly before looking back at her. "But I'm still not sure it's a good idea. If this is evidence in a crime, the police won't appreciate me messing with it."

"We don't know if it is or not," Janice backtracked. "That's what we're hoping to find out."

"I'm still not sure..." Stuart let his voice trail off. He considered his words for a moment, and then he continued. "Yes, I can take a section of the fabric to my other office"—Janice knew he meant the morgue, but he always tried to avoid saying that—"and I'll ask my friend at the lab to run the tests. They may find some DNA and they may not. But are you sure this is a good idea? I know you and your friends love the idea of a mystery. But maybe this is one case where it would be better to leave well enough alone."

Janice wasn't sure how to respond at first. She knew Stuart worried, and she was asking a lot. And maybe it was silly. It wasn't as if the girl who wore this dress was still in danger—if she ever had been in the first place—all these years later. But if the stain on this dress was evidence of a crime, if this did have anything to do with Peggy O'Neal's disappearance, or the drowning of Cynthia's sister, maybe they could help find answers. Even after all these years, surely the families would welcome answers about their daughters.

Then again, maybe it would turn out to be nothing—an even better outcome, as far as Janice was concerned.

"If you would prefer not to—"

"It's not that," Stuart said. "I can easily do some testing. I just want to make sure you're certain about this. In case there's something unpleasant at the root of all this."

"I'm not so worried about something being unpleasant," Janice said. "I'd rather know the truth. If there's any way this stain can help a family get answers about their daughter, I want to be a part of it."

Stuart weighed her words for a moment, and then he nodded. "All right. I'll see what I can do." He opened his desk drawer and pulled out a set of latex exam gloves and slipped them on. Then he opened the small drawer in the middle and pulled out a scalpel.

"You know, most people keep pens and paper in their desk." Janice laughed.

"Most people don't have my job." Stuart pulled the dress closer to him and turned the hem over.

"What are you doing?"

"Looking for a small section to cut away to test. I don't need to keep the whole thing. I was hoping I could get a section under the hem where it wouldn't be noticeable."

"Oh." Janice hadn't thought about that. That was thoughtful of him. "Okay."

"It looks like there's enough of this stain that I can cut a swatch from the underside of the hem," he said, and sliced off a square no larger than a postage stamp.

"Are you sure you took enough?" Janice asked.

"This is more than enough," Stuart said. He used a pair of tweezers from his desk to lift up the fabric and tucked it into a plastic bag. "You can take the rest of the dress back."

"Thank you." You couldn't even tell he'd made a cut from the front. Not that anyone would want to wear the dress again, not with that stain. But still. Janice wrapped the dress in the tissue paper and set it gently back in the plastic bag. She started to push herself up so he could get back to his patients when Stuart said, "I heard you met Dash last night."

Janice lowered herself back down. "You talked to Stacy?"

Stuart nodded. "She called this morning."

"He seemed like a nice guy," Janice said.

"He is a nice guy," Stuart said. "And he's good for Stacy. He makes her happy." Janice realized that Stuart had met Dash, and she felt a pang of jealousy. Why had Stacy introduced Dash to her brother before her mom?

"He seemed nice," she repeated, not sure what else to say. Surely Stuart couldn't think Dash was the right man for his sister?

"You should get to know him," Stuart said. "Look beyond the tattoo and the facial hair and the job, and get to know him as a person. If you give him a chance, you'll see that he's really great."

"I did give him a chance," Janice said.

"Ma." Stuart cocked his head. "I mean *really* give him a chance. Try to see what Stacy sees in him. I think you'll like him. I do."

Janice didn't know how to respond, so she said goodbye and left.

As she drove home, Janice was still replaying the conversation over and over in her mind. Why did Stuart think she hadn't given Dash a chance? Had Stacy told him that? What else had Stacy said about her? The thoughts stayed with her as she navigated the narrow streets, but as she got closer to the historic downtown area, with its cobblestone streets and arching trees, now bare and stark in the winter sunlight, she was distracted. These streets hadn't changed much since she was a child. Sure, some of the stores had changed hands, but the buildings themselves, the bricks and stones, had been here for generations. The trees had been here at least as long. The bookstore down there was a general store when she was younger, and the pizza place was a drugstore with a soda fountain where she'd spent many happy hours. But if you squinted, if you didn't look at the cars parked along Front Street or the clothing people wore, it could almost be fifty-plus years ago. It could almost pass for the era when that box was buried in their yard, when Peggy O'Neal had disappeared.

That had been such a big story when she was younger, and had scared so many parents into locking every window and forbidding their daughters to walk alone. Janice had been several years younger than Peggy, but she remembered the fear she'd felt in those days. It had been almost visceral, this terror that a bad man was hiding behind every corner, just waiting to abduct another girl. But now, all these years later, Janice realized that she wasn't really clear on all the details of the story. She knew the kidnapper had come in through Peggy's second-story window, taken her, and driven off. But what evidence had been left behind? Why hadn't her screams alerted the rest of the family? How had he gotten away with her without anyone noticing?

Janice knew she should get back to the inn, but she decided she had time to make one stop first. She turned on Washington, drove three short blocks, and parked in front of the Marietta County Library History and Genealogy Archive. Janice loved the main branch of the library, with its soaring ceilings and stacks and stacks of books just waiting to be checked out. But she knew that the newspaper archives were kept here, in this squat red-brick building perched at the top of a sloping lawn. Janice parked in the small lot and made her way inside the quiet building.

Janice waved to Danny, the librarian she'd met on previous trips. He was a nice guy, and delightfully, unabashedly nerdy in the best possible way, but Janice didn't need his guidance today. Her first step was the genealogical database, and she'd used that before.

She headed toward the back, where there were several computer stations set up that could access the archives of hundreds of newspapers and magazines around the country as well as databases of genealogical records. Filing cabinets lined the walls, filled with microfiche images of the pages of local newspapers. Janice sat down at one of the terminals and shook the mouse to wake up the screen, and then she opened the program that would allow her to search through the genealogy database.

She clicked on the tab for birth records, and, after some quick math in her head, typed in the years to search. If Peggy was seventeen when she'd disappeared, she'd been born in 1946 or 1947. There was no guarantee she'd been born in Washington County, but it was worth a shot.

Janice typed in the name Margaret O'Neal, and a moment later, the record came up. Margaret Michelle O'Neal, born January 17, 1947, to Douglas and Geraldine O'Neal at Marietta Memorial Hospital. There was only one record for that name. This had to be her.

Now that she knew Peggy's real name had been Margaret, Janice knew that the dress in the box could have been hers.

Which meant that the next step was to search the newspaper archives to see what else she could learn about the kidnapping.

She typed the name Peggy O'Neal into the search space and hit Return. There were hundreds of results. She clicked on the first link and pulled up the full text of the article from the *Chicago Tribune*. The story really had been a big deal if it had traveled as far as Chicago.

KIDNAPPING ROCKS SMALL TOWN
Peggy O'Neal was a normal seventeen-year-old girl, outgoing, gregarious, and involved in band and the spirit squad at the local high school. She loved her friends, her parents say, and

her church. Marietta, a small, tight-knit community on the banks of the Ohio River, was a safe place to grow up.

But the peace of the small town was shattered when Peggy O'Neal was kidnapped from her bedroom on Tuesday night, and the police say there are no leads.

Janice skimmed the rest of the article, but there wasn't a lot of actual information. She needed to find a newspaper account closer to home, she realized.

She looked through the links and found several articles from other regional newspapers, but they all seemed to have simply reprinted the article that was in the Chicago paper.

She needed to find the *Marietta Times*. The local paper would have covered the disappearance thoroughly, Janice was sure. She pushed herself up and wandered over to the filing cabinets that lined the wall. She thought the *Times* was over in this... She squinted at the labels on the drawers. There. She studied the dates listed on the sides of the cabinets and found the drawer that held the film for 1964 and 1965. She slid open the drawer and selected the box labeled June 1964. Then she sat down at the microfiche machine in the corner of the room and turned it on.

Microfiche had once seemed so cutting edge, she thought as she lifted the slides in the box, looking for the one that would contain the newspaper images for the days right after Peggy's kidnapping. It had seemed so much easier to use than microfilm and so much more efficient than keeping paper copies of every newspaper. She turned the dial at the side to focus the image on the large screen. When this technology was new, no one had even imagined that one day you'd be able to access a whole world of information on a computer that could fit in your pocket.

Janice moved the slide, looking for an image of the paper from later June. There. June 27, the masthead said.

STILL NO LEADS IN THE CASE OF PEGGY O'NEAL, the headline read.

Investigators are still baffled by the disappearance of Margaret Michelle O'Neal, who was kidnapped from her home on Second Street Tuesday night. The seventeen-year-old was last seen by her parents as she headed upstairs to her room after dinner and was discovered missing in the morning. Books, papers, and her bedding were found strewn across the floor, but there were no signs of forced entry on her second-story window, which was left open. A neighbor, identified as Paul LeBreux, recalls seeing a car idling in front of the house at around 10:30 p.m. the night Peggy disappeared, but cannot recall the make or model of the vehicle, and can only say that he thought it was strange.

Several people in the community have come forward to report sightings of an unknown man seen hanging around the local area in recent days. The man is described as being in his fifties and was reportedly wearing a long trench coat despite the heat. A source with knowledge of the case says police are searching for more information about who the man is and whether he could be involved in the disappearance.

"We urge anyone with information about what happened to our little girl to please come forward," Mr. Douglas O'Neal,

the girl's father, said. The family has offered a reward of $10,000 for information leading to her safe return.

Janice remembered hearing about the stranger now. She'd been afraid of men in trench coats for years after that. But had they ever found out who he was, or whether there was a link to Peggy's kidnapping? She needed to keep reading.

Janice moved the film back a bit and found the front page for June 24. LOCAL GIRL DISAPPEARS FROM BEDROOM, KIDNAPPING FEARED, the headline read. This must have been the first article about the case, Janice realized. She read the article, but there weren't many new facts in this one. She learned that Peggy's younger brother, a thirteen-year-old named Sam, who was sleeping in the bedroom next door, recalled being awakened by a crash, but he didn't get out of bed to investigate, and didn't realize his sister was gone until the next morning. Janice's heart broke for Sam. Could he have stopped the kidnapping if he'd gotten out of bed to see what the crash had been? Did he wonder about it after the fact?

Janice moved forward along the slide then, reading follow-up articles that had appeared in the paper the next few days. She found the page of the newspaper that had been in the box in the yard, and now she read the full article. No new leads. No idea who the mysterious trench coat man was. No clues as to whose car had been idling in front of the house. No real suspects. And then, on the fifth day, there was no mention of Peggy at all.

That was strange. Janice went back and looked through the pages again. Was she missing something? She looked at the front page for June 29. Surely there was something.... Well, maybe it had fallen off the front page, but surely there was something inside.... But there was nothing. No mention of Peggy in the newspaper at all that day. Janice moved on to the next day's paper, but again there was no mention of Peggy's kidnapping, and none on the following day either.

What in the world?

Had Janice simply remembered this kidnapping as the biggest thing to happen in town in years because of how much it had affected her? Was the disappearance outsized in her mind because of how strongly her own parents had reacted? Was it possible that it hadn't been such a big story after all?

Janice shook her head. She couldn't see any other explanation, really. The story had entirely disappeared from the newspaper in less than a week.

She thought for a minute, and then got up and found the slide that contained the newspaper for June 24, 1965—one year after the disappearance. Surely there would be some sort of remembrance or mention of the anniversary. But there was nothing.

Janice fed money into the printer and printed off copies of each of the articles, and then she pushed herself up. Well, that was less than enlightening, she thought as she moved toward the door. She waved goodbye to Danny and then headed back to her car. Had Peggy ever been found? Surely that would have made the news. But wouldn't it have continued to stay in the news if she hadn't been found?

Janice turned on the engine and cranked up the heater. All she'd discovered was that Peggy O'Neal's kidnapping had not been as big of a story as she'd thought it was. But did that mean that the items in the box weren't connected to her? The article about her kidnapping had been in the box, and her initials matched the initials on the dress's tag.

Janice didn't know what to think as she put the car in gear and drove back toward the inn. A few flurries fell, and they made it seem even colder, though the dashboard heater was starting to warm the chilly air inside the car. Janice tried to make sense of the abrupt end of the news about Peggy. Why had the papers just abandoned the story? A kidnapping of an upper-middle-class teenage girl was the kind of thing that would keep selling newspapers for weeks. So why did the story drop? Was there something more going on?

Janice decided to make one more stop before heading back to the inn. She turned on Putnam Street and pulled up in front of the two-story brick building that housed the Marietta Police Station. When she walked inside, a man with a paunch and a thick mustache looked up from his computer and asked in a lazy drawl, "How can I help you?"

"I was hoping to speak with Randy Lewis, please."

"Officer Lewis is out on patrol, but he's due back shortly. Do you want to wait?"

Janice didn't really want to wait, not with all the things she had to do piling up at the inn, but she didn't see any other option, so she settled into one of the plastic chairs by the door and started scrolling through the messages on her phone. There was an email from a friend who'd moved to Florida a few years back and an email from the church prayer chain for Jean, a woman who'd attended their church for decades. She was in the hospital again. Janice said a prayer for Jean, asking the Lord to heal her and help her. Maybe she could make some time to stop by and say hello. There was an email from her daughter-in-law-to-be, Zelda, who was out on tour with the Christian band she sang with. Then she turned to Facebook and scrolled through her feed, looking at photos of her friends' grandchildren and their puppies and record snowfalls in the north.

"Mrs. Eastman?"

Janice looked up to see Randy Lewis standing in front of her. Where had he come from? "Randy." She tossed her phone into her purse and stood up. "Hello."

"Hi there. Bob tells me you'd like to talk to me."

"I'd love to ask you a few questions if you have a minute."

"Of course." He gave her the same cockeyed smile that had gotten him out of so many scrapes as a child. "Come on back."

He pushed a button and the door to the back buzzed, and Randy pushed it open. She followed him past an open area filled with desks to a small conference room at the back. He sat down in a padded leather chair at one side of the round table and gestured for her to sit on the other side.

"I sent the knife to the lab, but I haven't gotten the results back yet," he said, and Janice was reminded that he'd visited the inn the day before, while she'd been at Stacy's. LuAnn and Tess had told him about the box and all the things inside it.

"That's great," Janice said, settling into the soft leather seat. "It's blood, by the way. I tested it myself. But that's not what I'm here about. Well, not exactly."

He tilted his head. "You tested it yourself?"

"With hydrogen peroxide. Not on the knife, obviously. But on the dress. It bubbles, which means it's blood."

"Okay...." he said slowly. "Well, our teams will use a more scientifically rigorous approach to testing the material." He shifted in his chair. "So what was it you wanted to talk to me about?"

"I was wondering if you could tell me about an old case. I don't know if it was ever solved."

"Huh." He leaned back in the chair and it groaned beneath him. "How far back are you thinking?"

"It was a kidnapping. In 1964."

"Is this connected to the knife you found?" he said with a smile.

"That's what I'm trying to figure out."

"Well, I can certainly check. What can you tell me about the kidnapping?"

"It was a seventeen-year-old girl named Peggy O'Neal. Margaret was her real name. She was kidnapped from her bedroom. I looked up the story in old newspapers, but I couldn't find anything that told me if she was ever found."

"Interesting." He wrote down the names and the dates on a yellow legal pad. "I'll see what I can find. It may take some time, and if I do find something I might not be able to tell you what it is, but I'll look."

"Thank you," Janice said, and pushed herself up to go. "I appreciate it."

Janice headed out and drove back to the inn. She was surprised to see that the plumbing crew was at work in the yard as she drove up. They must be freezing. But she was grateful. The sooner they had the plumbing issue resolved, the better.

Janice trudged inside the inn and found LuAnn chatting with the guests in the café while Robin, who worked part-time at the café and helped with the cleaning, was wiping down the tables with a rag.

LuAnn turned and waved, and Janice waved back and headed upstairs, where she found Tess on the couch, staring at a piece of notebook paper, her laptop next to her.

"How did it go?" Tess asked, looking up.

"All right." Janice set her purse by the door. "Stuart said he could do some testing to try to find out if there's any DNA in the stain on the dress, so hopefully we'll find something out that way. And Randy said he would look up Peggy O'Neal's case file."

"That's great." And then, a moment later, "You were gone a while." Tess didn't phrase it as a question, but it was clear that was what it was.

"I also stopped at the library annex." Janice walked toward the couch, and Tess moved her laptop so there was room for her to sit down. "To do some research on Peggy O'Neal."

"What did you find?"

"Well, her name was indeed Margaret, so points to you for picking up on that."

"I'll add it to my tally." Tess gestured for Janice to go on.

"And I read several articles about the case, including the full article from the one that was in the box."

"Did you learn anything?"

"She was kidnapped from her bedroom, like I remembered. There were signs of a struggle. A neighbor saw a car idling outside but nothing about the make and model. Her younger brother in the next room heard a crash but didn't go to investigate."

"How tragic."

"I know. I can't help thinking how that must have haunted him." Janice thought for a moment. "I had forgotten that there were reports at the time of a man in a trench coat seen around town. As far as I could tell, they never identified him, but there was speculation that he was involved."

"Ah. The mysterious stranger. Every mystery needs one of those."

Janice cocked her head and looked at Tess. "What?"

"It just seems a bit convenient, doesn't it? Something bad happens, and people always look for someone to blame. The stranger seems like an obvious choice. He shows up in a number of mystery stories, and most mysteries in real life, as far as I can see."

Janice didn't know how to respond.

"Just ignore me," Tess said. "Just because he's a literary trope doesn't mean he's not real."

Janice adjusted the throw pillow behind herself. "So you do think he exists? Or you think he's a fictional character?"

"I don't know, obviously," Tess said. "I'm sure people did really see someone they didn't recognize around town. But is there any indication he's related to the kidnapping? Or does he just get the blame because he's a stranger?"

"I think it was also the trench coat."

"You can never trust a man in a trench coat," Tess joked.

"It was June!"

"Maybe he had poor blood circulation."

Janice sighed. She was even more confused than she'd been when she started. "I don't know if he exists or not or if he had something to do with Peggy's disappearance or not. Or whether he had poor blood circulation. But I did find that the case completely vanished from the press within a week."

"I thought you said it was a big deal."

"It was. At least, I remember it being a big deal. But the papers dropped the story quickly."

Tess waited a beat before she said, "Doesn't that seem strange to you?"

"It does. But I don't know what to make of it." Janice sighed. "Anyway. What were you up to before I disturbed you?"

"All you disturbed me from was banging my head against a wall." Tess gestured to her computer. "I was looking up number sequences."

"Number sequences?"

"It's probably a waste of time, honestly. But I was looking at that dragonfly bracelet we found in the box. And I was interested in the numbers engraved on the inside."

"I thought we decided they were a birthdate."

"They might be. But I wanted to make sure we weren't missing anything by making that assumption, and I noticed that they were all square numbers."

Janice cocked her head again. She knew a square number was made when a number was multiplied by itself. "It was nine—"

"Three times three," Tess said.

"Twenty-five—"

"Five times five."

"Thirty-six."

"Six times six."

"Huh. I have to admit, I'd never in a million years have picked up on that."

"I'm not sure it was good that I did," Tess said. "Because I've just spent the past half hour researching number sequences."

"Did you find anything?"

"Just that some people spend way too much time on this stuff." Tess picked up her laptop and opened the screen. "There are some famous number sequences, like the Fibonacci sequence, which is where you find the next number by adding the two that came before it." She read off the screen. "So it's zero, one, one, two, three, five, eight, and so on."

Janice nodded. That sounded vaguely familiar.

"And there are progressions of squares. So one, four, nine, sixteen, etc."

"That would have been where our numbers fit, right?"

"Right. Except they don't. We have nine, twenty-five, and thirty-six. They're all square numbers, but they skip sixteen. And I can't find any pattern where that makes sense."

"So where does that leave us?"

Tess closed her laptop again. "Confused, mostly."

"You can say that again."

Tess was about to respond when her phone buzzed. Janice pulled her phone out and saw that they'd both gotten a text from LuAnn.

She's here.

Janice turned to Tess, but she was already texting back. *We'll be right down,* said the message that appeared on Janice's phone. Then Tess turned back to Janice. "You ready?"

"Ready for what? Who is here?"

"Cynthia."

"Cynthia?" Janice had heard that name recently, and she scanned through her memories, trying to place it. "The guest who stayed here in the fall? The one whose sister drowned in the river?"

"Right." Tess walked to the elevator and pushed the button, and the doors swished open. "Her parents owned Dudley's."

"She's downstairs?"

"She's downstairs." Tess put her hand against the door to hold it. "LuAnn called you."

"She did?" Janice looked down at her missed calls, and sure enough, LuAnn had called. Janice had the sound off, and she must have missed the buzz while the phone was in her purse. "Look at that. She did. What did she say?"

"Cynthia got LuAnn's message from yesterday and called back this morning to say she was driving over this way anyway today and could come by around one. Which is right now."

Janice stepped into the elevator next to her, and the doors closed. Was it really one o'clock already? No wonder Janice was hungry. Oh well. There was no time for lunch now. She'd grab something later.

"That's what got me thinking about the numbers in the bracelet," Tess said. "I was looking at it again because she was coming over." The elevator started to move downstairs.

"Let's hope she can give us some answers," Janice said.

The elevator doors opened, and Janice spotted LuAnn sitting at a different table in the café now, chatting with a woman with dark hair threaded with gray.

"Hi there." LuAnn smiled as they walked toward them. "Janice, Tess, do you remember Cynthia?"

"It's good to see you again," Tess said.

"Thank you so much for coming," Janice said. Cynthia had tortoiseshell glasses and wore a thick wool sweater over jeans. She was probably a decade younger than Janice, maybe more. She did look familiar, Janice thought, but she'd never really gotten the chance to talk to her like LuAnn obviously had.

"It was no problem," Cynthia said as Janice and Tess sat down. "Honestly, I would have come back just for the soup here." She gestured to a bowl of Winnie's cheesy potato leek soup on the table in front of her. "I had the chicken with rice when I was here before, and I thought that had to be the best I'd ever had, but this is even better. Is the food always this good?"

"Pretty much," Tess said with a smile.

They had worked hard to make sure the café served delicious, hearty breakfasts and soups that would keep customers coming back.

Janice's stomach grumbled. Tess laughed. "Why don't you get a bowl too, Janice?"

Janice didn't argue. She got up, went into the kitchen, and helped herself to a bowl of the thick, rich soup. Then she rejoined the others at the table.

"I really enjoyed my stay here, so I was happy to come back, but I have to admit I was curious when I got your message," Cynthia said. "LuAnn mentioned something about finding a box buried in the yard?"

LuAnn quickly explained about the box and the things they'd found inside. She'd brought the box downstairs and set it on one of the neighboring café tables, and she stood up now and pulled out the matchbook.

"I remember you saying your parents had owned Dudley's." LuAnn set the matchbook on the table in front of Cynthia.

"Oh, wow." Cynthia picked it up gingerly and turned it over in her hands. "I haven't seen one of these in years." She chuckled. "My parents had thousands of them in the garage when I was a kid. They were always trying to give them away."

That hardly seemed safe, Janice thought—thousands of matchbooks stored in a garage sounded like a recipe for disaster. But instead of saying so, she spooned soup into her mouth so she wouldn't say something she would regret. It must have been okay, she reasoned, since Cynthia hadn't mentioned the garage catching fire.

"So there were a lot of these matchbooks?" Tess asked. Janice saw where she was going with this—if there were a small number of matchbooks given out, maybe they would be able to trace where this one had come from.

"I would imagine so. They brought the leftovers when they moved to Cincinnati after they sold the place, but I assume they gave them out here in Marietta as well." She opened the cover and looked at the neat rows of matches and then closed it again. "But I wasn't born yet when they owned Dudley's, so I can't say for sure."

"When you stayed here, you explained to me why they left town," LuAnn said gently. "Would you mind telling the story to Janice and Tess?"

"Not at all," Cynthia said. She set the matchbook down, took another bite of soup, and then started. "Like I said, this all happened before I was born, so I didn't get any of this first-hand, but my parents talked about it often enough that I know the basic outlines."

LuAnn had already given them the backstory, and Janice braced herself for a heartbreaking tale.

"My parents married young, and they struggled for a while. My dad did construction, and my mom worked at the phone company. From what I understand, they made ends meet, but those were tough times. My dad started looking for extra work, and he ended up getting a job tending bar at a local dive. Apparently my parents kept it quiet from their families, because it wasn't exactly the kind of place you'd want to brag about, and well, their families didn't really approve. But the money was good, and by then my parents had moved away from their strict upbringings anyway, and well… There was a child on the way, so they needed the money."

"Your sister."

"My sister," Cynthia confirmed. "Lorelai."

L, Janice thought. Had Lorelai been the one to write those letters?

"Shortly after she was born, the owner of Dudley's was ready to move on, and he'd come to trust my father, so he offered to sell him the business."

"And he could afford to buy it?" Tess asked.

"I guess he'd been saving all his tips over the years, and he'd saved up quite a stash." Cynthia took another sip of soup. "I guess it was lucrative. He ended up buying the business and he ran it for a few years. Things were good, I understand. My mom had left her job when Lorelai was born, and Dad was able to drop the construction job and just run the bar. They lived above the bar, which—I can't even imagine how loud it must have been. And with a baby? But they made it work."

"Does he ever talk about what it was like?" Tess asked.

"Well, he passed away about five years ago," Cynthia said. "And we just lost Mom last summer. But they didn't say a lot about it, and I never really asked a lot. Talking about this time in their lives was always hard for them."

Because of what happened to Lorelai, Janice thought.

"I get the sense it wasn't the most upstanding place," Cynthia continued. "Though again, that's only what I've gathered from overheard comments from relatives and such. My parents certainly never came out and said anything of that sort. Like I said, they didn't really talk about this time very often."

"And that was because of your sister?" LuAnn asked gently.

Cynthia set her spoon down and broke off a piece of roll. "Exactly. It was pretty devastating for them."

"Of course." Janice nodded. "She drowned, right?"

"Yes. In 1962. She was only four at the time, and apparently she had wandered outside. There'd been a lot of rain, and the river had broken its banks. They'd told her not to go near the water, but apparently she was a very curious child. And well... By the time they realized she was gone, it was too late."

The currents in the rivers could be powerful and unpredictable on the best of days. Even very experienced swimmers had been lost in these waters, and if the water had been in flood stage...

"I can't even imagine," Tess said. Janice's stomach dropped just thinking about it. It was every parent's nightmare.

"They found her a little ways downriver," Cynthia said. "It destroyed my parents."

"How could it not?" LuAnn asked.

"I guess they tried to make a go of it here for another six months or so, but having to look at the river every day was just too hard."

"Is that when they moved to Cincinnati?" Janice asked gently. That meant they would not have owned the place in June of 1964, which was the earliest the box had been buried. So who had owned it then?

"Exactly. They sold the business for a song and moved back to my mom's hometown to start over."

"I'm so sorry," Janice said. What a terrible thing to live through.

"It marked them, for sure. Relatives told me they were never the same afterward. And you know, I have two kids myself, so I completely get it." She dipped the piece of bread into the soup and popped it into her mouth and then chewed before continuing. "That's why I came here. When I read about the inn, I decided this was my chance to see it for myself. I'd never been here, you know. My parents never wanted to come back. So I wanted to see the place where it all happened, and maybe understand it a bit better."

"Did your visit do that?" Tess asked.

"Yes. Very much so. The building where Dudley's was is long gone, I knew that, but this is about as close as you can get these days. It helped me to see it, to be able to visualize the place. And, well, I found such peace here. This inn is lovely. You three have done a tremendous job creating a beautiful place."

"Thank you," LuAnn said, speaking for all three of them. And then, "When you told me about all of this before, you mentioned that your sister had been wearing a bracelet when she...when the accident happened."

"That's right. A gold bracelet with her name engraved on it, surrounded by dragonflies. My parents searched everywhere for it, but they never found it."

Janice felt her heart sink. It wasn't the same bracelet. They had dragged this woman all this way and forced her to relive this awful part of her family's history, and it wasn't even her sister's bracelet.

Tess stood up and walked over to the box and took out the tarnished silver bracelet. "We found this in the box, and LuAnn mentioned that your sister's bracelet had never been found, so we hoped that maybe…" She held the metal circle out as her voice trailed off.

Cynthia took the bracelet and turned it over in her hands. "It's lovely," she said. "But it's not her bracelet." She examined the fine etching patterns and the tiny aquamarine stones. "I mean, I never saw her bracelet personally, but from what I understand, it was gold, and I never heard any mention of stones. Plus"—she held the bracelet up and studied the inside—"I don't know what these numbers are, a birthday maybe, but they don't mean anything to me. And this is far too big. She was only four."

Janice nodded. This silver bracelet was sized for someone much larger than a four-year-old.

"We're sorry to have dragged you here, then," LuAnn said. "We hoped we'd be able to reunite you with your family history, but…" Her voice trailed off.

Cynthia jumped in. "Oh, please don't apologize. I was driving past here on my way home from a work conference anyway. And I was glad for the opportunity to come back and spend some time in this beautiful inn. You three really have created a special place. And like I said, this soup is amazing." She laughed, and Janice looked down and realized that her bowl was already empty. Winnie really did do a great job in the kitchen every day. "And it's nice to be able to talk about all this. It's strange how much something that happened before I was born marked my life. I never really talk about it, and it's healing, in a way, to explore it all."

"We sure appreciate you making the trip," Tess said.

"I just wish I'd been able to help more," Cynthia said. "You've got an intriguing mystery here, and I wish I could have been some help in solving it."

Now that Janice knew how old Lorelai had been when she drowned, she saw how tenuous the link really had been. Even if it had been Lorelai's bracelet that they found, how would that help explain the rest of what they'd found in the box? The dress was clearly made for someone older than four, and a four-year-old couldn't have written those letters. And what about the blood on the knife, and the paper with the word *corona*? What could any of that possibly have to do with the accidental drowning of a four-year-old?

"You've helped us close one door, and that's always helpful," Tess said.

Janice nodded. What Tess said was true, but her mind was spinning, going over the items in the box one by one. They weren't just random items. There was a thread that connected them somehow. They just needed to find what that thread was. She thought about the matchbook and what it could possibly mean.

"I can't help thinking that Dudley's is important here," LuAnn said.

They all turned to look at her, so LuAnn continued. "I mean, the matchbook is there for a reason, right?"

"I don't know. It's hard to say much of anything for sure," Tess said. "But I like the way you're thinking. Keep going."

"I was just thinking. It seems likely we're dealing with something...unsavory here."

Janice noted that LuAnn chose her words carefully, not wanting to offend. Honestly, Dudley's had been seen as something of a cesspool, at least in the eyes of her church community, but she didn't dare say that out loud. "And when I was a kid, Dudley's didn't exactly have the best reputation," she offered.

"It's okay. You're not going to hurt my feelings," Cynthia said. "From what I understand, it was, as you say, unsavory. I mean, I don't think anything illegal happened there, but I get the sense that the people who hung out there were not always the high society types."

Janice nodded. "It did attract a certain crowd."

"After my parents started going to church, when I was a kid, they shared more about the tavern, and it sounds like it wasn't that great of a place."

Classic understatement, Janice thought.

But LuAnn continued. "Well, given that, I wondered if there would be any way to figure out how Dudley's was connected to all this."

"Hmm." Cynthia sat back in her chair and pressed her lips together. "I'm not sure. Like I said, both of my parents are gone, otherwise I'd ask them." She picked up her spoon and then set it down again. "You know, there are some boxes of old files and things in my parents' basement. I took a look at them right after Mom died, and from what I remember, some of them seemed like they could have been from this time. But I didn't look that carefully. And I haven't been able to face sorting through it all yet. But I could take a look and see if there's anything about Dudley's in there."

"That would be wonderful," Janice said. It didn't sound likely, but it didn't hurt to take a look.

"Even if it's just information about who they sold the tavern to. We'd appreciate it," LuAnn said.

Janice thought about Dudley's, about the rumors and quiet whispers she'd heard about the place as a child. About the things that might have gone on there, and about how it could be connected to how the box ended up in the yard. She also thought back to her morning, to Peggy O'Neal, and how she might figure out if she was connected to this in some way.

"My dad didn't like to throw anything away, so if he kept anything from the business, it would be there," Cynthia said.

"Thank you," LuAnn said.

They would just have to wait and see what Cynthia turned up.

CHAPTER SIX

May 18, 1861

Anna's fever had spiked that afternoon, and Prudence had spent many hours holding cool cloths to her forehead and wiping her body down with wet rags. The telltale red rash had spread. Scarlet fever. Anna hadn't been sure of her illness when she'd sent the message asking Prudence to come quickly, but there was no doubt of it now. Prudence tried to remind herself that many people who caught the fever survived.

"The box," Anna said in her delirium. "It's..." A pause, and then, "In the barn."

"Yes, Anna." Prudence dipped the rag in the basin of cool water and laid it on her forehead. Anna had been talking about this box for a while this afternoon, and Prudence did not know what she was talking about. Anna probably didn't know either, Prudence thought. Fever ravings.

"The hayloft..."

"Yes, Anna."

Anna was the closest thing to a mother she had. This was the woman who had taken her in, had raised her as her own. Who had taught her about God and the saving work of grace. Prudence would do whatever she could to nurse her back to health.

"Promise me," Anna said.

"Yes, Anna, I promise."

At these words, Anna's body seemed to relax, and finally, eventually, she drifted off into a fitful sleep.

While Anna was sleeping, Prudence went out to the barn to tend to the animals. She tossed out food for the chickens and shoveled out Doxology's stall. The old work horse nickered and let Prudence run her fingers along his muzzle, and then she tossed in some fresh straw. Then Prudence milked Hephzibah, and she carried the bucket of warm milk out to the icehouse. She went back to the barn to close the door for the night, but her eyes went to the hayloft.

Anna didn't know what she was saying. Why would there be a box kept up there? Prudence almost turned and walked away, but she'd promised Anna. Slowly, grudgingly, she climbed up the wooden ladder to the haymow. Her long skirt scraped on the treads and caught on her shoes, but she made it up and looked around. Evening light was streaming in through the cracks between the wooden slats, but it was still dim as Prudence looked around.

Nothing but hay. Prudence picked up the pitchfork that was leaning against the wall and used it to feel along the edges of the haymow and underneath the hay. Clouds of dust rose up, but there was nothing there.

Prudence rested the pitchfork back against the wall and carefully made her way down the steps. Anna must have been remembering something from her childhood, or some other time. There was no box here.

After Cynthia left, Tess made a trip to the grocery store, and LuAnn checked in another set of guests, a couple who were in town to meet their new granddaughter for the first time, while Janice dusted and ran a load of laundry. But by midafternoon, all three were gathered in the sitting room on the fourth floor, discussing where Cynthia's visit left them.

"They're not her things," Tess said. "The bracelet wasn't hers. She's not involved in this."

"I know they're not." LuAnn was slicing a butternut squash for soup for tonight's dinner. "But I still feel like Dudley's has to be connected somehow. Maybe her parents were involved, or something."

"Maybe," Janice said, dunking a tea bag in hot water. Tiny wisps of steam curled up off the surface. "But even if they were, they're gone. They've both passed away. Besides, they sold the business in 1962. How could they possibly have been involved if they were living in Cincinnati at the time?"

"I don't know." The knife made a loud thwack as it hit the cutting board. "I guess we need to find out who bought it from them. Maybe that's the connection, the people who lived there after them. I can't help but think that's where we need to be focusing our energy. After all, the box was buried in what would have been the yard for Dudley's at the time, right?"

"I think so," Janice said, but she wasn't sure exactly. "I think the old buildings were over that way." She gestured out the window at the back of the inn. "Along the alleyway. I'm pretty sure."

Tess shook her head. "I don't really know. I can't picture how this was all set up."

"Maybe we need to find out more about where the buildings were so we can make sense of this," LuAnn said as the knife hit the cutting board again. *Thwack.*

Part of Janice thought LuAnn was clinging to the idea that Dudley's was the key a little too hard. But part of her was curious too. If the box had been buried in what was then the tavern's yard, maybe it did make sense to dig into this a little more. But she didn't know how to go about that. "How?"

"I bet the historical society would have some information." *Thwack.* "Margaret had all that information about the inn and its history. Maybe she has something about the buildings that used to be behind it."

Thwack. It almost seemed like LuAnn was taking out her frustration on the squash.

Janice glanced at the clock. The historical society would still be open for a couple more hours.

"I think you should go," Tess said. "And leave that poor squash alone. What did it ever do to you?"

LuAnn laughed and set her knife down. "You know, maybe you're right. Maybe a trip to the historical society would help me calm down."

"And it would be safer for all the vegetables," Tess said.

LuAnn moved to the sink and rinsed her hands under the faucet. "Does anyone want to come with me?"

"Not me," Tess said. "I haven't had enough coffee to be able to handle Margaret today."

"Oh hush. You know she's not that bad," LuAnn said. "She just puts up a gruff front."

Tess sighed. "You're right, of course. But I'd prefer to stay here and get some laundry done."

"I'll come," Janice said. She wanted to understand the configuration of the buildings on the lot, and Margaret would no doubt be able to help.

"You two go then," Tess said. "I'll hold down the fort here. And I'll have soup waiting for you when you get back."

A few minutes later, LuAnn and Janice were walking into the Washington County Historical Society. The old wooden floors creaked as they stepped inside. Margaret Ashworth was bent over a table in the front room, and she looked up as they came inside. Around her were piles of yellowed hardcover books with faded cloth covers.

"Hello, Janice, LuAnn." Her white hair was caught up in a messy bun, and her eyebrows were penciled in in a rich mocha color. A slash of bright pink lipstick completed the look.

Margaret looked so tiny standing there, but Janice knew better than to think of her as diminutive. Margaret Ashworth could fill a room. "What can I help you with?"

"We were hoping you might be able to help us learn a bit more about the history of the land around the inn," LuAnn said. "Specifically, the stretch of old buildings that used to run along the alleyway."

"Those old death traps?" Margaret said. "I think I do have some information about them somewhere."

"Death traps?" Janice asked.

"Oh, they probably didn't start out that way. I think they were originally built as housing for workers down at the docks. But they were built cheaply, and over time they were subdivided and walls were put up inside and no one was really paying attention. That wasn't a great part of town forty years ago, you know. Your beautiful old inn was a warehouse most of the time those buildings stood. Hard to believe now, isn't it?"

Janice and LuAnn nodded, and Margaret continued. "Well, eventually there was a fire one night, back in the late seventies or early eighties, I would guess. I'll have to dig to find out for sure. Of course the buildings weren't up to code, and they went up quickly. Spread to the buildings on either side, and those went up too. Two people ended up dying in the fire."

"That's awful," Janice said. How did she not remember this? She supposed it all happened around the time that she had two young children, which meant that she spent her days in survival mode, and the world around her barely registered.

"It was terrible," Margaret agreed. "After that they tore the buildings all down. For a while it looked like Fred Martin was going to face charges, but I suppose that when you have that much money there are ways to get out of things."

"Fred Martin?" LuAnn said, repeating the name under her breath. Janice knew LuAnn had heard the name before and was trying to place it.

But Janice recognized the name immediately. "Irene Bickerton's husband." Irene and her sister Thelma were in their late eighties and early nineties, and they lived in a beautiful old home in the historic district that technically belonged to their nephew Brad Grimes, LuAnn's beau.

"Oh." LuAnn's eyes widened. "I always forget that her last name isn't actually Bickerton."

"She does like to remind people that she's a Bickerton," Margaret agreed. "But yes, her last name is Martin. She was married to Fred Martin for decades."

"And he owned the buildings behind the inn?"

"He did indeed. Was something of a slumlord, to be quite frank. People were always complaining that the heat never worked, the electricity would go out, the plumbing was bad, that kind of thing. But the rent was cheap enough that the apartments were always full." She shrugged. "If the fire hadn't happened, they would probably have fallen down of their own accord soon anyway."

"Do you have any records about those old buildings here?" LuAnn asked.

"I'm sure I do," Margaret said. "You'll just need to give me a minute to find them." She began to stack the books. "Is there anything in particular you're looking for?"

"We're hoping to find information about a tavern called Dudley's and the building it was housed in. Specifically, the yard for that building."

"Dudley's, huh?" Margaret shook her head. "You two really are hitting all the highlights."

"You know it?"

"I know *of* it," Margaret clarified. "I certainly never went there. It wasn't the kind of place our people went."

Janice didn't have to read between the lines to understand what she meant.

"It was named after Dudley Woodbridge, of course," Margaret said. "One of the first merchants in the whole Northwest Territory."

"But is there any indication that he had anything to do with the buildings behind the inn, or the tavern named after him?" Tess asked.

"I would imagine not," Margaret said. "He would have been well over a hundred years old by the time those buildings were erected. But if you're interested in learning more about Dudley's, I'll go see what I can dig up." She turned and walked down the hallway toward the back of the building.

"That's interesting that Fred Martin owned them," LuAnn said as soon as Margaret was out of earshot.

"It does make you wonder," Janice said. "It sounds like he didn't do a lot to care for his properties."

"No, it certainly doesn't." LuAnn let out a long breath. "It doesn't mean that he's involved in this, of course. It sounds like he didn't pay a lot of attention to what was going on in his buildings, but that doesn't mean he's guilty of anything except bad management. But we'll see what Margaret turns up."

LuAnn told Janice about the new guests who'd checked in that afternoon—retired science teachers from a suburb outside Pittsburgh. LuAnn always enjoyed talking to other retired teachers, and she told Janice all the differences between the school where they'd taught and LuAnn's own school in Clarksburg, West Virginia. Janice half listened, knowing LuAnn was just chattering to fill the time. The other part of her mind was thinking about what Stuart had said this morning, about how she hadn't given Dash a chance. Was there any truth to what he'd said? And even if there wasn't, would Stacy ever believe her?

"I found a few things," Margaret said as she walked back into the room carrying an armload of binders.

"Let me help you." Janice hurried to take some of the binders from her, but Margaret shook her head.

"I've got it," she said, and set them down on the table. "Now. You wanted to know about the buildings behind the inn." She flipped open the cover of one binder, and Janice saw that it was a collection of historic photographs of Marietta. Each photo was encased in a plastic sleeve. Margaret turned the plastic pages gently, and she stopped when she found a black-and-white photo of a building with half a dozen men with long aprons and handlebar mustaches lined up on the dirt road in front. Janice gasped.

"Is that—"

"That's the inn," LuAnn said, a smile spreading across her face. "I remember seeing this photo when we bought the place."

It looked like a totally different building, with a scalloped false front, but Janice could still see the familiar shape of the brick building beneath it. "Wow. That's crazy."

"It's fascinating to see how things change, isn't it?" Margaret said, and she kept turning the pages. Janice saw a photo of a streetcar driving down what looked like Front Street and pictures of gorgeous old homes and buildings. Then Margaret stopped and pushed the binder toward them.

"Here," she said. "These were the buildings."

The black-and-white photo showed a row of adjoined wooden three-story buildings. In contrast to most of the other buildings in the photos, these had no decoration, no shutters or trim to hide their stark white fronts.

"This was taken in 1945," Margaret said, pointing to the date etched in the corner. "The buildings were fairly new then, I think. At least, they weren't falling down yet, like they were later."

That explained why they looked much more pleasant than her memory of these buildings.

There were storefronts on the ground level of two of the buildings, while it looked like the others had apartments on all their floors.

"Where was this taken?" LuAnn was squinting, no doubt trying to reconcile this photo with the scene today.

"At the end of what's the alleyway now," Margaret said.

LuAnn nodded. Janice could see it too.

"This is where Dudley's was, though in this photo it looks like it was a laundry." Margaret pointed to the building that was second from the left. "And this"—she pointed to a rectangle of brick just peeking over the top of the building toward the right—"is the fourth story of what's now the inn."

Janice understood. That would put the front of the buildings along the alleyway, and the backs about fifty yards, Janice guessed, from where the inn stood. A live oak that now stood tall and proud at the corner of their property was about three feet tall in the photo.

"Is there any way to see what the back of the buildings were like?" Janice asked.

"Let me see." Margaret continued to flip through the binder of photographs, but she didn't find anything more, so she moved on to the next binder, which appeared to be a collection of old plat maps. "There has got to be something in here," she said. Janice watched as Margaret flipped through the pages, each drawn with lines that carved the town up into owned sections. Janice knew that these maps were drawn up by the city and used for tax purposes, so they were kept up-to-date.

"Okay," Margaret said, after a few minutes of searching. "This looks right." She pushed the binder toward them, and Janice and LuAnn bent over the map, trying to make sense of what they were seeing.

"This map is from 1958," Margaret said, and Janice nodded. That was the date stamped at the top. "This right here looks like the inn, right?" She pointed to a parcel of land along the riverfront. There was a number in the box, no doubt corresponding to a tax ID number of some sort, but it meant nothing to Janice.

"That's right," LuAnn confirmed.

"And these must be the buildings you're interested in," she said, pointing to a square of land that bordered what was then the inn's land. On a more modern map, the line between the properties would have been erased as they owned the whole section of land now. "It's all one parcel for tax purposes, even though there are five buildings on it," Margaret said.

Janice tried to picture where the box had been dug up. It was hard to tell exactly where the buildings would have been, since the plat map only showed the plots of land, not the buildings, but if the buildings had been right along the road... Janice thought back to where the workmen had been digging, The spot they'd found the box was probably not too far behind the buildings.

LuAnn must have been doing the same calculation in her head. "It was right about here," she said, pointing to a spot just a bit to the left of where Janice had guessed.

"Which would probably make it right behind the buildings," Janice said.

"Which means that it was very likely buried in the Dudley's backyard," LuAnn said.

"What was?" Margaret looked from Janice to LuAnn and back again.

Janice wasn't sure she wanted to bring Margaret into this, but she realized it might already be too late to do anything about that.

"Some workers were digging in our yard yesterday," LuAnn said. "And they found an old metal box buried in the ground. Right about here was where they found it." She pointed to the spot on the map.

Margaret's eyes widened. "What was in the box?"

"A whole bunch of stuff we can't make sense of," Janice said. "We're trying to figure out who might have buried it and why."

"Was there anything valuable in it?"

"No," LuAnn said. "It's more... Well, judging by the things in the box, it sounded like someone was in trouble. And we're hoping to find out what happened."

"In trouble?"

Janice realized Margaret was going to keep asking questions until they told her what they knew, and she decided it probably couldn't hurt to tell her.

"Here," LuAnn said, pulling out her phone. They had all used their phones to take photos of the box and of each object inside of it. "This is the box." She held out the phone, and Margaret bent over the screen to take a look.

"It looks like an old security box," she said.

"That's what we thought," Janice said. "It was locked, but we got it open."

"If you swipe, you can see it from different angles, and also photos of all the things that were in the box." LuAnn handed Margaret her phone. Janice could see that the first photo showed the letters from L.

"Those appear to be letters written by someone whose initial was L. to her mother. They were never mailed," Janice said before Margaret could ask.

"One of the letters made it seem like L. was in trouble, which is part of why we're concerned," LuAnn said.

"Gracious." Margaret swiped to the right and saw photos of the newspaper, the paper with the word *Corona*, and the knife. "Goodness. I assume this bloody knife is another reason?"

"That's right," Janice said. Margaret swiped to the picture of the newspaper and used two fingers to zoom in on the date. "I guess you know this wasn't buried before June 25, 1964," she said.

"That's right," LuAnn said. "Convenient that they included that, isn't it?"

"I'm not sure I'd say convenient," Margaret said. "Is that blood there too?" She pointed to the dark stains on the newsprint.

"Yes," LuAnn said. "The knife was wrapped in that."

"How awful." Margaret studied the paper a bit longer, and then she swiped to the next photo.

"Huh," she said, looking at the dress.

"Huh?" Janice repeated. Something in Margaret's tone was different.

"That's a Lilly Pulitzer," Margaret said.

"Right," Janice said, maybe a tad more excitedly than was strictly necessary. "That's what the tag said."

"We weren't sure if that was the designer or what," LuAnn said.

"Oh yes. She has a very iconic look. Most of her dresses are in these bright colors and fun floral patterns. They're recognizable. My niece and her friends were very into Lilly Pulitzer when they were teenagers."

"Your niece?" Janice asked. They knew Margaret had helped raise her niece and that she had passed away not too long ago.

"Not Dahlia's mother," Margaret said. "This is my oldest brother's daughter, Bronwyn. She was my first niece, and I always felt a special bond with her. I used to spoil her and take her around like she was my own daughter. Dahlia's mother came to live with me after Bronwyn was already in college."

Janice couldn't remember being into any designer when she had been a teenager. Come to think of it, she couldn't say she'd been a fan of any designers as an adult either. Designer clothes cost far too much, and you could get perfectly nice clothing at more reasonably priced stores.

"The next picture shows the tag," LuAnn said, and Margaret scrolled to the right. Janice could see the words *Lilly Pulitzer* printed in a script font in pink. The next photo showed the back side of the tag.

"M.O.," Margaret said under her breath. She paused a moment, looking at the photo of the tag and then scrolling back to the picture of the dress. "This was buried in the same box as the other stuff?"

"Yes," Janice said. Margaret was thinking about something, she could see.

"So this dress would have been from around that time. Or slightly before." Margaret zoomed in on the photo of the dress, looking at the pink and green flowered print, and then zoomed out again.

"That seems to be a fair assumption," LuAnn said.

"Huh," she said again. Janice could see that she noticed the stain at the hem but didn't say anything about it.

"What are you thinking?" LuAnn asked.

Margaret didn't answer for a minute, just continued to look at the dress. Then, slowly, she opened her mouth.

"I was thinking about Marilyn Oshmann."

"Who is Marilyn Oshmann?" Janice asked.

"Bronwyn had a group of friends from the stables, and Marilyn was one of them. They were all into Lilly Pulitzer," Margaret said, as if that explained everything. Janice struggled to understand how this was all connected.

"Do you think this might be her dress?" she asked.

"I don't know," Margaret said. "Just that it could be. But…"

That's when Janice noticed that Margaret's face had paled. "What is it?"

Again, Margaret waited a moment before she answered.

"It's probably nothing," she finally said. "It's probably a totally random coincidence."

"But…" LuAnn said gently. "Why don't you tell us what you're thinking, just in case?"

Margaret took in a deep breath and let it out slowly. For a moment, Janice was worried she was going to have a stroke or something. She wasn't exactly a spring chicken. But then she started talking again, and her voice seemed a bit more normal. "Well, Bronwyn's friend Marilyn, you see, she…" Another breath in, and out. "She disappeared right around this time. I'm not sure of the exact date, but Bronwyn was in high school, so it would have had to have been in the early to mid-1960s."

"What do you mean, 'she disappeared'?" Janice asked. She hadn't heard about this. Surely she would have heard about it if another teenage girl in Marietta had gone missing in the same year as Peggy O'Neal. It would have been front-page news.

"I mean, she quietly left town," Margaret said. "Or, at least, that was what we all assumed. The story was that she was going to go live with relatives in London for the school year, but she never came back after that. And the way it happened so quickly, and so quietly, well…" Margaret's voice trailed off. "You know Dahlia's mother lived with me for a while… and why she left town."

Janice and LuAnn nodded. A few months back, they had met Margaret's great-niece, Dahlia, the daughter of the niece who'd gotten pregnant and skipped town while she was living with Margaret.

"After that, I knew the signs."

"Ah." Janice knew that "going to live with relatives" was code for getting pregnant out of wedlock.

"I know that now people have babies without getting married all the time, but back then it was much more serious," Margaret said. "If a girl got in trouble, she was often shuttled away before she started showing to protect her reputation. I assumed—we all assumed—that was what had happened with Marilyn."

"And maybe it was," Janice said. When Stacy had turned up pregnant six years ago, she and Lawrence had floated the idea of sending her off to live with Janice's cousin in Iowa, but Stacy wouldn't hear of it. She'd said she was a grown woman, not some meek teenager, and she wasn't embarrassed. She claimed that the only reason they'd wanted her to go away was to spare themselves the embarrassment of the pastor's kid getting pregnant out of wedlock. All these years later, Janice could see that there was probably some truth in that, but she'd also—mainly—been concerned for Stacy. Nevertheless, Janice saw Margaret's point. If Stacy had been born a generation earlier, she likely wouldn't have had a choice. She would have been sent off to spare everyone the embarrassment, and the baby would have been placed up for adoption.

"But maybe it wasn't," LuAnn said.

"But how would her dress have gotten buried in this box with all these other things?" Janice asked.

Margaret shrugged. "That's what has me worried. There doesn't seem to be a good scenario where that could have happened. Maybe she didn't just go off to have the baby somewhere else. What if something happened to her?"

Janice could see that LuAnn was thinking through the possibilities, but Janice wasn't quite ready to go down that road yet.

"It's possible," she said. "But the only connection seems to be the dress. Surely there was more than one person with the initials M.O. who had a Lilly Pulitzer dress."

"Of course it's possible," LuAnn said. "But that's not the only connection."

Janice cocked her head, waiting for LuAnn to go on.

"The stables," Margaret said. "Bronwyn knew Marilyn from the stables. The newspaper had an article about the stables."

Janice realized she was right. That article about the jockey had spent several paragraphs talking about the stables associated with Hillsborough Racetrack. She must have been so focused on the second half of the Peggy O'Neal story that was on the page that she'd glossed over it. But could that possibly be the reason this page of newspaper was included in the box? Janice didn't know.

"And I'm pretty sure Marilyn's uncle, Roger Morris, owned Dudley's around this time."

"Wait. Really?"

"I'd have to check on the exact timing. But I think that's right. He bought it sometime in the sixties, I'm pretty sure. Roger and I... Well, he was sweet on me in high school. He was always the black sheep of that family, you know."

Janice tried to figure out how to make sense of this.

"Do you know how to get ahold of Roger?"

"Oh, he passed away many years ago, I'm afraid. Heart problems."

"Is there anyone else who might know about Dudley's at this time?" LuAnn asked.

"Hmm." Margaret thought for a moment. "I don't know. Our people didn't really have anything to do with that part of town."

"Of course not," LuAnn said. "Is there any way to get ahold of Marilyn?"

"Not that I know of," Margaret said. "As far as I know, she went off and never came back." She thought for a moment, and then she said, "I guess I could call Bronwyn to make sure."

Janice knew how easy it was to be clueless about exactly what was going on in your kids' lives, as Stacy's pregnancy had shown so clearly.

"Yes, why don't you give her a call? Maybe we'll find out that Marilyn Oshmann is alive and well and doing fine," Janice said. "And she'll be able to tell us whether or not this is her dress."

"But in any case, it will be good to know," LuAnn said. She pulled a notebook out of her purse, and Janice saw that she'd already begun keeping a list of the facts of this case. Under the heading *Girls* LuAnn had written *Peggy (Margaret) O'Neal* and *Cynthia's sister Lorelai,* but she'd crossed the second one off, no doubt after Cynthia's visit earlier today. Now, she took out a pen and added *Marilyn Oshmann* to the list.

"I'll give Bronwyn a call tonight," Margaret promised. "She just lives over in Williamstown." That was a town just across the river, on the West Virginia side. "I'll let you know what she says."

They thanked Margaret for her help, and then they headed out. Janice's mind was swirling, trying to make sense of everything they'd learned that day, but at this point, it just seemed like nothing made sense.

After dinner that evening Janice sat down to work on the jigsaw puzzle again. LuAnn was reading on the couch, and Tess was in her room. She fit a few pieces of the hydrangea bush into place, but she was distracted. Despite all the things that had happened today, the thing that her mind kept going back to was her conversation with Stuart about how she hadn't given Dash a chance. Hadn't she?

Janice tried to tamp down the doubt that kept creeping up. She realized she hadn't thanked Stacy for dinner last night. That would be a good reason to talk with her, Janice thought. Or—well, maybe a text was better.

She got up and retrieved her phone from where it was charging on the counter. She opened the text app and tapped Stacy's name.

Thank you for dinner last night! Janice typed. She went back and took out the exclamation point but then reconsidered and put it back in.

It was great meeting Dash. He seems like such a nice man.

There. That was true. There was no denying that he was nice.

Give Larry a hug for me, she added.

Janice read the message over. There was nothing Stacy could find objectionable in that, she thought. She hit SEND.

A moment later, the screen said the message was delivered. Janice waited a moment, and then she saw the three little dots on the screen that indicated Stacy was typing something in return. Janice kept her eyes on the screen, waiting for the message to come through. But the dots stopped moving and then disappeared altogether.

Janice waited, but the dots didn't come back. She watched until the screen went dark. Finally, she went back to her puzzle, but she kept glancing over at the screen, hoping to see a message from Stacy pop up. But there was nothing.

Finally, Janice turned the phone over so it wouldn't keep distracting her. Whatever Stacy had wanted to say, she wasn't saying it tonight.

CHAPTER SEVEN

The sun was shining when Janice woke up Saturday morning, and the sky was a clear, cloudless blue. She shivered as she stepped out of bed and wrapped a flannel robe around her shoulders. Though it was sunny, it was still frigid. She padded into the sitting room and found Tess huddled over her laptop, looking at pictures on her screen.

"Crowns?" Janice asked, leaning in.

"Just picking out my tiara for when I marry Prince Charming," Tess said. "There's coffee."

"Bless you." Janice took down a mug and poured herself a cup. "Let me guess. Still working on *corona*?"

"It has to mean something," Tess said. "I was hoping seeing pictures of crowns would spark something. But…nope."

"There are worse things to look at online." Janice added milk and sugar and stirred, and then she took a sip. Heaven.

"True, but there are better ways to spend my time." Tess closed her laptop and pushed it away. "Before I got lost looking at tiaras, I did find an obituary for Roger Morris."

Janice tried to place the name.

"Marilyn Oshman's uncle," Tess said. "The one who bought the tavern after Cynthia Cook's parents left town."

"Oh. That's too bad."

"It doesn't mean that we can't get any information about what happened that night. Just that he won't be able to tell us."

"Well, at least we know."

Tess pushed herself up. "LuAnn is already downstairs. I should probably go help her, since the Waltons are set to check out after breakfast, and another couple is supposed to check in later."

"Give me time to finish my cup of coffee, and I'll go strip their bed," Janice said. "And then do you want to go on a fact-finding mission with me?"

"A fact-finding mission? Where?"

"I want to start off at Antoinette's Closet, and then I thought I'd mosey on over to Harlowe's on Putnam."

"The jewelry store?"

"Exactly."

"Sounds like a shopping trip more than a fact-finding mission. Is someone feeling spendy?"

"I wish." Janice laughed. "Actually, I was thinking we could learn a bit more about the dress at Antoinette's and see if Emma can tell us anything about the girl who wore it."

"Ah. Good thinking. If anyone knows vintage clothes, it's Emma."

"And then I was hoping someone at the jewelry store would be able to tell us something about the bracelet."

"I see." Tess picked up her laptop. "Well, it certainly beats my plan for the day, which was hiding out under my quilt and praying for spring."

Janice knew very well that Tess had more than that planned. She was supposed to babysit her grandkids later and had stayed up late last night making cookies for them. But Janice laughed anyway.

"Count me in," Tess said.

Two hours later, Tess and Janice set off for Antoinette's Closet, the vintage shop set in the storefront of an old brick building just a few blocks from the inn. Normally they would have walked the short distance, but the frigid temperatures drove them to take Janice's car, and after they pulled up in front they hurried inside. The walls were lined with racks of clothing from all eras, and the back had a display of shoes and purses. Janice had spent time in plenty of thrift stores—married to a pastor, you had to be thrifty—but this store had more of a collection of interesting and brand-name clothes from the past.

"Hello, Janice, Tess," Emma called as they walked in. "Welcome."

Janice couldn't see her for a moment, but she then popped up from behind a rack of coats.

"Are you ladies looking for anything in particular today?" she asked. Emma had black hair that came down to her waist, and today she wore a long-sleeved navy dress with swans on it that looked like it came from the sixties.

"Actually, we were hoping you would be able to help us with something," Janice said.

"What is it? I'm glad to help if I can."

Janice spotted a display of vinyl records on a table next to a record player in a leather carrying case. Her father had something just like it when she was in high school.

She reached into her purse and pulled out the plastic bag, and then carefully unfolded the tissue paper and took out the pink and green dress. As it unfurled, Emma's eyes widened.

"Oh my goodness. Is that Lilly Pulitzer? It's vintage, isn't it?"

"We believe so," Tess said. "We were hoping you might be able to tell us about it."

"Oh wow." Emma reached out for it. "Can I see it?"

"Please."

Emma took the dress and held it up, studying it.

"It's gorgeous. That stain is unfortunate, but you might be able to get it out, and it would be worth even more. Even as is, I think it would sell for a decent price."

"We're not really looking to sell it," Janice said. "We were more hoping you could tell us something about it."

"Like what?"

"For starters, who in the world is Lilly Pulitzer, and why is everyone so excited about her dresses?" Tess asked.

Emma laughed. "Okay, we can start there for sure. Lilly Pulitzer was a socialite who started a clothing line in the early 1960s."

"Is she, you know, a Pulitzer, like the prizes?" Janice asked.

"I think so, but I'm not sure." Emma shrugged. "All I know is that her clothes typically have bright, colorful, floral prints, and they've always been popular with preppies and socialites."

Well, that explained why Janice had never heard of them. She wasn't exactly vacationing on the Vineyard or attending charity balls.

"And the vintage styles, especially if they're in good condition, are highly desired by collectors." Emma gave them a significant look.

"Can you tell anything about the person who owned this dress by looking at it?" Tess asked.

"Let me see." Emma gestured for them to follow her to the counter at the front of the store and draped the dress over it. Janice noticed that there was a display of small, ornate ladies' hats, complete with feathers and flowers, on a table next to the register. She couldn't think of any occasion to wear a hat like that unless you were attending a wedding of a member of the British royal family. But Emma knew what she was doing, and she must sell them if she stocked them.

"This is a size fourteen," Emma said, looking at the tag. "Which would be more like a six or an eight today."

"Hold up. What?" Tess asked.

"Vintage sizing is a little tricky, because years ago, clothing manufacturers started their sizes at six or eight, not zero."

"Ah. Right. Vanity sizing," Tess said.

Janice cocked her head.

"Women wanted to be smaller sizes, so manufacturers didn't make the clothes smaller, they just made the size number smaller," Tess said.

"Exactly," Emma said. "Marilyn Monroe was famously a size fourteen, but she wasn't a fourteen by today's standards. She would probably wear a size eight today. It's just a different way to label clothes."

"So you think that whoever wore this dress was reasonably slim," Janice said. She didn't need Emma to tell her that. She could see that just by holding up the dress.

"Yes, and my guess is that she was also on the younger side. Past a certain age, it's hard to pull off these bright patterns."

Easy for her today when she was in her twenties, Janice thought. But she saw Emma's point.

"This brand typically appealed to people with a bit of money, and still does today. Which is why you should let me sell this dress," Emma said with a smile. "I could help you get that stain out."

"If we do decide to sell it, you'll be the first to know," Janice promised. "For now, thank you for your help."

"Any time."

Janice wrapped the dress back up and slipped it into the plastic bag, and then she and Tess turned to go.

Back in the car, Janice said, "Well, she didn't really tell us anything we didn't know."

"Except that whoever wore this dress wasn't poor," Tess said.

"Right. Except we kind of already knew that too. Margaret said her daughter's friends from the stables were really into this brand. How many kids without money do you know who ride horses?" Janice put the car in gear and pulled away from the curb. It was only a few blocks to the jewelry store, but it was too cold to walk.

Secrets of Wayfarers Inn

"True," Tess said. "So Marilyn Oshmann no doubt came from a wealthy family."

"And Peggy O'Neal's father was the president at the bank."

"Right. What we don't know is how a rich girl's dress ended up stained with blood and buried in a box behind a seedy tavern."

"There's one other thing we don't know," Janice said.

"What's that?"

"Who in the world is Antoinette?"

Tess laughed. "I assumed it was named after Marie Antoinette. Marietta is named after her, you know."

"I know that," Janice said. "But really. Do you think Marie Antoinette would have worn that black sequined number Emma had on display?"

"I suppose we'll never know."

Janice pulled into a spot in front of Harlowe's Jewelers. The store had been here for decades and was now run by Melissa Harlowe, the granddaughter of Benjamin Harlowe, who opened the store back in the fifties or sixties. Janice had only been inside a few times, but she knew this was where Lawrence had picked out her engagement ring. He'd saved for it for months, and she'd been so proud to wear it. Now it was tucked safely away in her jewelry box at home.

Janice held the door for Tess and then followed her inside. Glass cases ringed the room, and gems and sparkly baubles glinted in the overhead lights. A bell rang over the door as it closed and Melissa Harlowe came out of the back wearing a loose, flowered top and dark slacks.

"Hello, Janice," she said, smiling as she saw who it was. Many years ago, Melissa had been part of the choir at Christ Fellowship, but Janice hadn't seen her there in quite some time.

"Hi, Melissa. Have you met my friend Tess? She and I run Wayfarers Inn, along with our friend LuAnn."

"It's nice to meet you, Tess." She held out her hand. Melissa was probably in her forties now, Janice realized. "It's pretty incredible what you all have done with that building."

"We enjoy it," Tess said.

"So what brings you in today?" Melissa asked. "Are you looking for anything in particular?"

"I'm afraid we're not here to shop," Janice said. "We were hoping you could help us with something."

"What's going on?"

Janice reached into her purse and pulled out the dragonfly bracelet, which she'd tucked into a plastic sandwich bag. "We're wondering if there's anything you can tell us about this."

"Let me see." Melissa reached out and took the bag, and then she carried it around one of the glass cases and set it down on a black velvet tray. Then she pulled on a pair of white cotton gloves and slipped it out of the bag before she pulled a headband on and tugged a magnifying lens down over one eye.

While she studied the piece, Janice looked at the jewelry on display. There was a lovely white-gold cross with a tiny red stone in the center. Garnet, she guessed. And she liked some of the simple silver necklaces down at the far end of the case. Tess, meanwhile, had wandered over to the section where diamond tennis bracelets and necklace charms were on display. Tess turned and saw her, and shrugged. "A girl can dream, right?"

"It's silver plate," Melissa finally announced.

"Not sterling?" Tess asked.

"I'm afraid not. And these stones, I think they're aquamarine, though I can't tell for sure. So probably not extremely valuable, but it's very pretty. The dragonfly etchings are lovely."

"Can you tell anything about when it was made, or where?" Janice asked.

"I don't recognize the design, so I'm guessing it wasn't made by one of the big designers," she said. "But judging from the art deco style, I'd say there's a decent chance it came from the twenties, thirties, or forties." She turned the bracelet over. "What about these numbers? Do you know what they are?"

"We guessed a birthdate, but we don't know for sure," Janice said.

"That would be my guess as well," she said. "Do you know whose?"

"That's what we're trying to figure out," Tess said.

"Got it." Melissa turned the bracelet over again, studying it under the magnifying lens. "I'm not sure how much more I can tell you, I'm afraid. But it truly is a lovely piece." She shoved the headband up so the lens was on the top of her head. "I could repair the clasp for you if you'd like."

Janice and Tess looked at each other.

"Thank you but not right now," Tess said.

"Would you like me to polish it for you?" Melissa asked.

Janice glanced at Tess again. Did they want that? Would it ruin whatever authenticity there was, or destroy any potential clues?

"Sure." Tess shrugged. "If you don't mind, that would be great." She turned to Janice and continued. "I don't see how it could hurt to see it looking like it did when someone wore it. Maybe it will spark some new direction."

"I suppose you're right," Janice said.

A few minutes later, the bracelet gleamed in the plastic bag. Janice didn't know if it would spark any new direction of their thinking, but it sure looked a whole lot better.

"That was interesting," Tess said as she buckled herself into the car.

"How so?"

"She didn't come right out and say it, but the bracelet is cheap. Inexpensive stones, silver plate instead of sterling."

"I wouldn't say that makes it cheap, necessarily."

"Well, right. It's still silver jewelry. But it's not exactly what you would expect from someone who wears Lilly Pulitzer, if what Emma said was accurate. If that's a high-end preppy brand, wouldn't you expect the owner of that dress to wear a bracelet of sterling silver, not silver plate? And diamonds or sapphires instead of aquamarine?"

"I suppose." Janice saw the point she was making, but she wasn't sure she was ready to concede that there was a contradiction. "The bracelet is probably older than the dress. Maybe it's an heirloom, and the family came into money later."

"Or maybe they don't belong to the same person at all," Tess said.

"I don't know," Janice said, letting out a sigh. "I thought finding out more about the dress and the bracelet would help us make sense of that box, but it's really just left me even more confused."

"Make that two of us," Tess said with a smile.

Janice pulled away from the curb and started back toward the inn, navigating through the crowds that were starting to pick up even on this frigid Saturday morning. Before they made it to the corner, her phone began to ring in her purse.

"Want me to dig it out?" Tess asked, and Janice nodded. Maybe it was Stacy. But when Tess looked down at the screen, she said, "Marietta Police Department."

"Oh. Can you answer it?"

Tess swiped the screen and put the phone to her ear. "Hello, Janice Eastman's phone."

Janice tried to hear the other end of the conversation but couldn't make it out over the hum of the motor. All she could hear was Tess saying, "Really?" and "That's interesting." And then, just before she hung up, she said, "Great. We'll be right there."

Janice flipped on her blinker and pulled over into the right lane before Tess had even hung up the phone. "To the police station?"

Tess nodded. "Randy said you'd asked for some information about open missing persons cases from the 1960s. He found something and wants you to come check it out."

He'd found out something about Peggy O'Neal. Janice felt her heart pounding in her chest as she turned onto Putnam Street and drove the short distance to the parking lot behind the police station. This time, she was shown right in, and a few minutes later, they were sitting in the same conference room where she'd sat just yesterday.

"Thanks for coming so quickly," Randy said as he sat down next to Tess.

"We're anxious to hear what you found," Janice said. She had explained the situation to Tess as they drove over.

"Well, see, that's the strange thing," he said. "I looked into that file you asked me about. The Peggy O'Neal case?"

Janice nodded.

"And I found something strange. I can't tell you if the case was ever closed."

"Why not?"

"Because I don't know. The files were sealed."

"Sealed?" Janice asked at the same time that Tess said, "Well, open them."

He laughed. "I'm afraid I can't just open them. It would take an order from a judge to get the case files unsealed, and there would have to be good reason."

Janice wanted to argue that they had a good reason, but she suspected the police wouldn't see it that way. Not without further evidence that the box they'd found was connected to the case.

"Why would it have been sealed?" Tess asked.

"I really don't know," Randy said. "This isn't something I've really encountered before. But I checked with Chief Mayfield, and he said in no uncertain terms that we cannot open those files."

"Interesting," Janice said, trying to make sense of what he'd said. "When were they sealed?"

"I don't know."

Janice thought about this. What possible reason could the police have for sealing the records? Unless they knew what happened to Peggy, and there was someone they wanted to protect. Were the police somehow involved in this?

"I'm sorry I couldn't be more help in this case," Randy said. "But I did some more digging, and I did come up with another case involving a young woman from around that time period that was never closed."

"Really?" Janice asked.

Randy nodded. "The remains of a girl named Lidia Jankowski were found at the base of the Harmar Bridge in the summer of 1964."

"Ugh. How awful," Tess said.

"Wait. Really?" Janice had never heard of Lidia Jankowski.

"Really. She was sixteen."

"Oh my goodness." Tess shook her head. "I can't even imagine."

"It's a pretty tragic story, honestly." He pushed a file folder across the table toward them. "I made a copy of the file for you, but the gist of it is that she went off at night to meet a boyfriend and was stabbed to death."

"Some boyfriend," Tess said.

"They never did find who did it," Randy said. "But hey, if anyone can solve a fifty-five-year-old case, it's you guys. Maybe you'll see something in here our guys missed all those years ago."

Janice took the file, but her mind was still unsettled. Not just about the murder of a teenage girl, which was tragic enough. But somehow this poor girl had been killed not too long after the Peggy O'Neal kidnapping, in the same town, and Janice had never heard her name. Had she just missed it? How had that happened?

She kept turning the information over in her mind as they walked back to the car.

And was poor Lidia connected to the box they'd found?

"Not to point out the obvious, but Lidia starts with *L*," Tess said as she buckled herself in. Janice nodded. She'd realized that. Was it possible that Lidia Jankowski had been the *L* who'd written the letters that were in the box?

"Let's take a look at the file when we get home and see what we find," Janice said. Whatever was in that file, she was almost afraid to find out.

It was a few hours before Janice finally had a chance to take a look through the police file. Robin had called in sick, so Janice and LuAnn had both helped served lunch in the café while Tess attended to the laundry and took care of some billing. Then Tess went out to babysit her grandchildren—four-year-old trip-lets—and once the café was cleaned up and things had calmed down, Janice and LuAnn headed upstairs.

"I forgot to tell you I called Irene Bickerton—Martin—this morning," LuAnn said as she grabbed her purse. She had a date with Brad tonight, and she was headed out to get her hair done. It looked fine to Janice, but LuAnn insisted that it needed a trim and a blowout, and who was Janice to argue when it came to her hair?

"About the buildings her husband used to own?" Janice asked. She glanced over at the puzzle on the card table. She hadn't gotten very far in the past day or so. But then her eyes were drawn to the folder of information about the Lidia Jankowski case.

"Yep. She was running off to something but invited us to come by tomorrow afternoon to discuss them."

Janice enjoyed the image of elderly Irene running off anywhere. "So we've been summoned?"

"Pretty much." LuAnn dug through her purse to find her car keys. "But I figured that it was the only way we were going to find out more about those buildings. Are you free?"

"Of course." Even if she'd had something scheduled, Janice would have cleared her calendar for this. Maybe Irene knew something about how the box had ended up in their yard.

"Great. Oh, and Margaret Ashworth called. She talked with her niece Bronwyn and gave her our number, and she's supposed to call sometime soon." LuAnn unplugged her phone, tucked it into her purse, and then started down the stairs. Janice, left alone, picked up the folder of police information and sat down at the table with it.

As soon as she started to read, she wished someone else were here to verify that she was seeing what she thought she was seeing. Could this be for real?

CHAPTER EIGHT

May 19, 1861

The doctor arrived shortly before noon. Prudence had sent for him when Anna's fever had spiked again, and all of the herbs and compresses and tinctures Prudence tried did nothing to bring it down. She did not know how she would be able to pay him for his services, but she would worry about that later.

"Let me see," Dr. Randolph said, setting his black leather case down next to the iron bedstead. His mustache twitched as he looked Anna over, taking in the marbled pink rash and her sweaty, waxy skin. "How long has she been like this?"

"I arrived Monday night. She has gotten worse since then."

He examined Anna carefully. "You did right to call. She needs to be bled immediately."

"Bled?"

"To let out the bad humors." He sat down on the chair by the bed. "Do you have a bucket handy?"

After Prudence had given the doctor the tools he requested, she retreated to the sitting room. She was sure the new technique was a medical advancement, but she could not stand to see it.

Prudence looked around the small room. Anna had been raving again this morning, talking about that box again, asking Prudence to find it. She said something about not forgetting. Prudence hadn't been able to understand what was supposed to be inside, just that it was important to Anna. Well, she had some time now. She would search the house, from top to bottom. If that box was here, she would find it.

Prudence searched in every cupboard and behind every piece of furniture. She even looked under the loose board, the hiding spot Anna thought she didn't know about. There was nothing inside but a thick roll of dollar bills and a velvet pouch with some baubles. Well, that would help with the problem of paying for the doctor, but it could not be what Anna had been talking about.

Prudence didn't know what else to do. But she supposed that if it was all that important, the Lord would lead her to it.

Saturday evening LuAnn was rushing around upstairs getting ready for her date with Brad while Tess and Janice spread everything from the metal box out on the coffee table in the lobby. Their guests had gone out for the evening, so there was no danger of them stumbling upon the scene. Their plan was to try to see all the objects at once and hopefully find a connection they'd been missing. They had cleared the coffee table of the photo books that normally sat there and carefully laid out the box itself as well as the dress, matchbook, paper, letters, tablecloth, newspaper, and bracelet. Stuart still had the knife, so Janice drew a picture of it and cut it out and set it among the other things, just so they didn't forget about it.

"I don't know," Tess said, studying the items. "If there's some obvious connection here, I'm totally missing it."

"I don't know what I was hoping we'd find," Janice said with a sigh. Wasn't this what they did in mystery novels? They took everything all in at once, and suddenly the answer became clear? "I thought that if we saw it all spread out like this something might jump out at us. But you're right. I'm not seeing anything."

"I mean, I see a dress that maybe belonged to Marilyn Oshmann, or possibly Peggy O'Neal, or maybe Lidia Jankowski, or maybe someone else entirely. There are letters from someone with the initial *L* written to a mom who never got them. There's the matchbook from a dive bar behind where the box was buried, though no one knows why, and there's a paper with the Latin word for *crown* of all things written on it. There's a cheap but pretty bracelet with some numbers we don't understand engraved on the inside. A newspaper probably stained with blood that ties the other objects to several people. And there's a very convincingly drawn paper pocketknife."

Janice laughed. "At least you had something positive to say about my drawing."

"The real version of which, by the way, is stained with what's probably blood too."

"Yep, and that's not funny." Janice looked around again. "That about sums it up, in a typical straightforward style." She sighed. "Well, it was worth a try."

"I'm sorry, Janice." Tess pushed herself up from the couch. "I'm tired. Those kids wore me out this afternoon. And I think I'm hangry."

"Let's get these things back upstairs, and we can have dinner. And I'll tell you what I learned about the Lidia Jankoswki case while we eat."

"Sounds perfect. Nothing like an unsolved murder to whet your appetite." And then, a moment later, Tess added, "I'm sorry. I'll be in a better mood after I eat something."

Janice stood up when the doorbell rang. Tess waved her off and went to get it, and Brad stood at the door holding a bouquet of stargazer lilies for LuAnn.

"Those are lovely," Tess said, ushering him inside.

Janice loved how well Brad treated LuAnn. Her friend had been through enough heartache, and she deserved to find a man who treated her well.

"I'll tell LuAnn you're here," Janice said, dashing off a text to LuAnn. LuAnn texted back, promising to be right down.

"What's all this?" Brad asked, looking at the items spread out on the coffee table.

"We're not sure," Janice said. "We found all this stuff locked in a box in the yard. It looks like it's been there since the sixties, and we're trying to figure out whose stuff it is and how it ended up there."

Brad nodded, but as he looked around at the objects on the table, his gaze stopped on something. Something in his face changed. Janice tried to figure out what he was looking at, but as soon as she opened her mouth to ask, the elevator dinged, and LuAnn stepped out.

"Hello there," LuAnn called. Her hair did look good, Janice had to admit, sleek and smooth, and she wore a dress in a flattering shade of blue. She had a fine wool coat and a cashmere scarf and her purse draped over one arm. But Brad hadn't even noticed. He was still staring at something on the table. "Are you ready to go, Brad?"

Saying his name seemed to snap him out of whatever reverie he'd been in, and he smiled and held out the flowers.

"Hi, LuAnn." As she stepped closer, he leaned in and gave her a peck on the cheek. "These are for you."

"They're lovely." She took them and looked around, and Tess stepped forward and held out her arms.

"I'll put these in water for you," Tess said. Janice got a whiff of the deliciously sweet scent as Tess took the flowers from LuAnn. "You two have a good time."

"Thank you," LuAnn said, and she slipped one arm into her coat. Brad helped her get it over her shoulders, and then they turned toward the door. Before they stepped out, though, Brad turned back around and took one last glance at the table. His forehead wrinkled, and then he faced away from the table and went out the front door.

As soon as the door closed behind them, Janice turned to Tess. She'd set the flowers down on the piano bench and was starting to put things back into the metal box.

"Did you see that?"

"Did I see what?" Tess folded the newspaper up carefully and set it inside.

"Brad."

"Yep. I saw Brad. I said hi to him, remember?"

"No. I mean, did you see the way he froze when he saw something on the table?"

"Uhhh... Nope." Tess stopped and looked at Janice. "What was it?"

"I don't know."

"Do you know why?"

Janice shook her head. "But I swear I saw it. Something on this table meant something to him."

"Okay." Tess didn't sound like she totally believed Janice, but she was willing to play along. "Should we stop them and go out and ask him what?"

"I'm sure they're already gone," Janice said.

"Probably better not to spoil their date anyway," Tess agreed.

"But I'll find out," Janice said.

"All right. But for now, can you help me put these things away so we can go upstairs and eat?"

A few minutes later, they were sitting down at the table in the kitchenette on the fourth floor. Janice had made chicken and rice, one of her favorite recipes, and it had only taken a few minutes to warm up the frozen rolls.

Tess shoveled a bite of casserole into her mouth and then did it again.

"My goodness. Those kids must have really worked you hard today," Janice said.

"I told you I was hungry." She took another bite, chewed and swallowed, and then continued. "I feel like I ran a marathon. I basically chased them around the house for three hours."

"You know, most grandmothers do quiet, genteel things like bake cookies with their grandchildren," Janice said.

"There are three of them," Tess said. "Three four-year-olds. Have you spent time with a four-year-old recently? I am not taking them into any room with knives."

"Maybe a movie and popcorn?" Larry loved when they did that. Though he'd gone through a Thomas the Tank Engine streak for a while there that had tested even Janice's patience.

"One of them is constantly up, needing to use the bathroom or wanting a snack or water. I have to pause the movie every time, and an hour-and-a-half film takes five hours."

"I guess chasing them around is your best option, then," Janice said with a shrug. "Take seconds."

Tess helped herself. "Okay, now that I'm having some food I'm feeling calmer. Tell me what you learned about Lidia Jankowski," she said.

Janice took a bite. After she'd taken a sip of her water, she spoke. "The police file wasn't especially thorough," she said. "From what was there, I learned that Lidia was alone with her older sister at the time of her death. The mother had gone back to Poland to bury her father."

"What about Lidia's father?"

"He was interviewed, but he wasn't living with Lidia and her mother. His name was Jacob Opalinski, and he already had a family." She took another sip of water. "Lidia's mother was 'the other woman.'"

"Ah." Tess took another bite of rice. "Lidia was the result of an affair."

"Apparently. But he appears to have known about Lidia and sent some money each month, though it was very little."

Tess chewed her bite, thinking it through. "So if Lidia was the L. who wrote the letters, that part lines up. Her mom was far away. Okay. So, so far it seems possible she's our girl. So what happened?"

"The sister Karolina says Lidia was there when she went to bed, but she was not in the apartment when she got up at 5:00 a.m."

"5:00 a.m.?"

"She apparently had a job cleaning and cooking for some rich family in town, and she was expected to be there early."

"So she called the police."

"And the police didn't come out right away. Apparently they didn't believe anything was wrong at first. They chalked it up to a girl sneaking out to have some fun, to maybe meet a boyfriend, and assured Karolina that she would come home soon enough."

"But she didn't."

"No. They changed their tune pretty quickly when Lidia was discovered under the bridge later that morning."

"Yikes."

"She'd been stabbed by a short knife of some kind."

"Okay. So far this is lining up in truly horrible fashion. Could the knife in the box be the one that was used to stab poor Lidia?"

"But they never figured out when she left the apartment or who she'd gone to see in the night."

"There were no signs of a struggle in the apartment?"

"None. All signs indicated that she left that apartment by her own will," Janice said.

"What did the sister think?"

"She didn't know. The police seem to have operated on the theory that she'd gone to meet a boyfriend. But no one ever came forward—"

"Of course not."

"—and Karolina said Lidia wasn't that kind of girl."

Tess snorted. "Wouldn't she have hidden it from her older sister if she were?"

Janice shrugged. "Karolina insisted that it didn't make any sense that she would have been going to meet a guy, because she was wearing an old dress and her work shoes."

"Hmm."

"She apparently had much nicer and newer dresses in her closet. 'Why would she wear her old clothes if she was going to meet a guy?' Karolina said."

"She had a point. Do you know any woman who would wear junky old clothes to meet up with a guy she was interested in?"

"I know LuAnn got her hair done and was wearing a new dress when she walked out the door tonight."

"Exactly." Tess pointed her fork at Janice. "So I don't think I buy the boyfriend theory."

"Well, apparently the police did, because it seems they didn't look too hard to find any other reason she might have gone out at night."

"Right. Because what other reason would a woman possibly have for doing something except for a man?" Tess said, rolling her eyes. "Okay. So let's go with the theory that it was a boyfriend. They must have talked to Lidia's friends, right? What did they say? Did they know who he was?"

"She didn't seem to have had many friends, but the few they talked to didn't know of a boyfriend."

"And yet the police still insisted that's what happened?"

Janice shrugged.

"What about the dad?" Tess asked.

"He was the obvious suspect. He and his wife had been having money trouble, and the wife was threatening to leave if things didn't change."

"So the obvious solution is to get rid of his daughter?" Tess shook her head. "To save the pittance he sent to her mother every month?"

"It doesn't matter. We know he didn't do it, because he had an iron-clad alibi."

"Which was?"

"He was at Dudley's all night. Drank too much and passed out, and Roger Morris put him to bed on a couch upstairs."

"Dudley's." Tess shook her head. "There it is again."

"Like a bad penny."

"And Roger verified this?"

"A dozen people saw Jacob there past midnight, and then saw him slink to the floor. Roger and his wife Meredith testified that he was there snoring until eight o'clock in the morning, when she finally kicked him out."

"He sounds like a charming guy."

"A cheater and a drunk, apparently. But not, it would seem, a murderer."

"So who did kill her?"

"The police never found out."

"Hmm." By this point, Tess had polished off her second helping of chicken and rice and two rolls. "I guess what confuses me most about all of this is the fact that you'd never heard of her."

"It confuses me too. Like I said, everyone in town was freaking out about the Peggy O'Neal kidnapping, but I don't think I'd ever heard of Lidia before today. Why wasn't this an even bigger deal than Peggy? It should have been."

"Is it possible it was, and you just missed it?" Tess set her fork down on the edge of her plate. "You were, what, eight? Maybe your parents shielded you from it."

"Sure, it's possible," Janice said. "It does seem like the kind of thing you would try to keep your young child from hearing about. Maybe that's what happened. I guess I would need to go to the library annex again and look through the newspaper archives to see for sure. Or maybe there's a more obvious explanation."

"You think the cops were in on it?" Tess asked.

"No. I mean, sure, I guess it's possible. But what I was thinking was, this was the daughter of a poor cleaning lady. One who, according to the notes in the file, didn't speak great English. A girl whose father, a drunk, had another family."

"While Peggy was the daughter of a bank president."

"Maybe kidnapped rich girls sell more papers," Janice said.

"And get more attention from the police," Tess added. "From what you said, it seems like they didn't exactly pull out all the stops to try to find the killer."

"The investigation just sort of slowly petered out, from what I can tell," Janice said. "Would the same thing have happened if Lidia had been the daughter of someone with more money and privilege, with a more traditional family structure?" It was a horrible thing to think, but Janice wasn't naive about how the world worked.

"Except that you said the Peggy O'Neal story stopped running in the papers," Tess said.

"And I don't know if the police stopped investigating it or not, or really anything, because the records were sealed."

It didn't make sense. None of it made any sense. They both sat quietly for a moment, thinking. And then Tess said, "So, do you think this is Lidia's stuff we found in that box? Or, at least the dress and the bracelet?"

"I think there are enough links to the things in the box that we should add her to the list," Janice said. "But we'll have to do some more research to figure out how her things would have ended up here." She picked up the last bite of her roll. "How about you? Did you turn up any more possibilities for the word *corona*?"

Tess said no, and explained all the different meanings she'd tried to make sense of. Janice listened, but because she'd already heard the same basic explanation from LuAnn, a part of her was far away, thinking back through the text she'd sent to Stacy last night. What had Stacy been planning to write back? Should Janice send her another text? Would that get her to respond?

"What's bothering you?" Tess asked.

Janice snapped back to attention. "I'm sorry. I'm listening. I promise."

"It's okay," Tess said. "I would probably zone out listening to someone explain about the ring of the sun's light during an eclipse too. But something is bothering you. I can see it in your eyes."

Janice didn't often find herself getting emotional, but she couldn't help it now. She felt tears sting the corners of her eyes.

"I guess there is something bothering me," she said. "I mean, it kind of seems silly considering the gravity of what we were just talking about with Lidia. It's nothing terrible like that."

"But it's bothering you, and that makes it important," Tess said. "What is it?"

Janice took a deep breath and tried to get her breathing under control before she answered. "It's Stacy."

"What's going on with Stacy? Is she okay? I thought you said the dinner the other night went well."

"It did go well. At least, I thought it did." Janice used the side of her fork to cut a last bite of chicken in half. "I guess it's just that Dash wasn't exactly what I was expecting."

"Oh dear."

Janice popped the chicken into her mouth. She chewed it, thinking. It had tasted so delicious a few minutes ago, but now it kind of tasted like cardboard.

"He's an artist."

"Okay...."

"It's hardly a stable career choice."

"The way you set that up I thought you were going to say he's a serial killer or something. Given that, an artist doesn't sound so bad."

"He uses found objects."

"Okay...."

"That's trash."

"Is his art the main thing you didn't like?"

"No. He's also got these weird earlobe stretcher things. And a tattoo of some kind of scary flaming bird on his arm."

"A phoenix?"

"I don't know. Maybe? Who cares?"

"I would think you would. A phoenix is an ancient symbol of resurrection. Did you ask him what his tattoo means?"

"What his tattoo means? It means he's got an ugly tattoo."

Tess's head was tilted. "I'm waiting for you to say something about his character. That he's mean to Stacy, or treats Larry badly, or something like that."

"Well, no. He was perfectly nice. But what man wouldn't be pleasant meeting his girlfriend's mother? Of course he was nice."

There was a pause, and Janice couldn't keep it in any longer. "What kind of name is Dash, anyway? That's a punctuation mark, not a name."

"Did you ask him about it?"

"No."

"Maybe you should. There may be an interesting story there."

"Maybe." Janice set her fork down. She wasn't hungry anymore.

"Stacy seemed to like him?"

"Yes," Janice said. "Very much."

"She was excited enough about him to invite you over to meet him."

"Yes. And now Stuart tells me she's upset because I didn't give Dash a chance."

"It kind of sounds like you didn't."

"That's not true. I—"

But Tess held up her hand.

"Janice, you know I love you, right?"

Janice nodded slowly.

"Then please don't take this the wrong way."

"Oh dear. In my experience, that means what follows is definitely going to be hard to hear."

"Believe me that I say this with love. You can sometimes be a tiny bit quick to make judgments."

Janice let the words sink in. Everything in her wanted to argue against them, but she knew Tess wouldn't say them if she didn't believe they were true. And Tess knew her better than just about anybody.

"I know that your relationship with Stacy is…complicated," Tess said.

Janice nodded. There was no denying that. She still wasn't sure how it had happened. When Stacy was born, Janice had felt a love like nothing she'd ever experienced. Sure, she'd fallen head over heels for Stuart when was born, but there was something different about holding her baby girl. She imagined frilly Easter dresses, mommy-daughter tea parties, whispering over cute boys. She'd been so full of hopes or their relationship. But Stacy always chose Lawrence, even as a little girl, and she always seemed to push Janice away. They'd butted heads from the beginning, and the teen years had been especially hard. Maybe they just had very different personalities. Maybe she'd been too strict. Maybe living in the fishbowl of a pastor's family had been too much for Stacy. Maybe Janice had pushed too hard. Even when Janice had lived with Stacy and helped her take care of Larry, there had been a distance between them. Janice had chalked it up to the exhaustion of new motherhood, but maybe that wasn't all it was. She didn't know. All she knew was that she would give just about anything to have a better relationship with her daughter.

"And it seems like she wanted to introduce you to a man who had become a part of her life."

"Yes. I suppose I didn't realize how big a part."

"I think it's a good sign for your relationship that she wanted you to meet him. It probably hurt her that you didn't warm to him like she hoped you would."

Janice thought about what Tess was saying. As much as she wanted to deny it, she realized it was probably true.

"So what should I do?" she asked.

"It sounds like you should probably apologize to her," Tess said.

Janice took in a deep breath and then let it out.

"You're probably right."

"Of course I am. I'm always right."

Janice let out a laugh, but it came out sounding more like a sigh. She was being childish, and she knew it.

"And then I think you should get to know Dash."

Janice nodded.

"I'll give her a call."

CHAPTER NINE

Sunlight streamed into the inn on Sunday when Janice and LuAnn came home after church. Tess had gone to have lunch with Jeff Jr., and Janice was looking forward to lunch and maybe a nap before they were supposed to go talk with Irene.

"Welcome back," Robin said as they took their coats and scarves off.

"Thank you for holding down the fort," LuAnn said. "Was everything all right?"

"Just fine. Both couples that were staying here had breakfast. But otherwise it's been pretty quiet. You got a phone call."

"Who was it?" Janice asked.

Robin walked over to the check-in desk where the phone sat and consulted a small notepad. "It was from Bronwyn Meyers. She said her aunt, Margaret Ashworth, asked her to call you."

"Oh, great." Maybe she'd be able to tell them something about Marilyn Oshmann. "Did she leave a number to call her back?"

"She sure did. It's here."

"Thank you, Robin."

"Anytime."

They went upstairs and ate a quick lunch of sandwiches, and then LuAnn settled down on the couch with her book.

Tom settled in right beside her, purring as he kneaded the blanket. Janice called Bronwyn back, but the call went straight to voice mail. Janice left a message with her phone number, and then she looked around. She could spend a bit of time working on the puzzle, or she could make that call to Stacy she knew she needed to make. But her bed was calling to her. Maybe just a short nap, and then she'd get ready to go. But just as she was pulling back the covers, her cell phone rang.

Stuart, the screen read.

"Hello?"

"Hi, Ma. I stopped by the office—"

"On a Sunday?"

"One of the patients I saw this week was getting worse, so I needed to see her right away."

Janice could see that this was a good excuse and showed how kindhearted he was. But it still didn't sit well that he was working on a Sunday, the only day he was guaranteed to have off each week. Maybe Zelda would get him straightened out once they were married.

"In any case, when I came in I picked up a voice mail from my friend at the lab. She had the test results ready."

"Oh. From testing the fabric?"

"Yep."

"What did you find out?"

"I was hoping I could come by and return the swatch and show you in person. Do you have some time now?"

"Sure." The nap could wait. "I'm here for the next hour or so. Come on by."

"I'll be there in a few minutes."

Janice roused LuAnn from her book, and a few minutes later they met Stuart downstairs. He carried the scrap of fabric in a plastic bag, and he pulled a folder of papers out of his briefcase.

"You were right that it is indeed blood," Stuart said. Janice felt a brief moment of satisfaction that she'd told him so, but it quickly turned to frustration. They already knew that. Was that all he was going to tell her?

"It's type A positive," he continued.

LuAnn nodded, but Janice wasn't sure how that could help them. Unless they had a way to find out what blood type Peggy O'Neal, Marilyn Oshmann, and Lidia Jankowski were, that didn't really help much.

"Can you use DNA to tell whose blood it is?" LuAnn asked.

"If we had a sample to compare it to, we might be able to," Stuart said. "But without that, not really. There's not some big library with samples from people sitting around out there—"

"Thank goodness," Janice said.

Stuart nodded. "So without something to compare it to, I'm not much use there."

"What about the person's ethnicity?" LuAnn said. "I thought DNA samples could be used to tell things like where a person is from."

"Ah. You mean like those services where you take a sample from your cheek with a cotton swab, send it in, and they tell you where your ancestors came from?"

"Exactly."

Janice saw where LuAnn was going with this. If the test came back with a strong Polish background, they would have a very good reason the blood might belong to Lidia Jankowski.

"That kind of test may be possible, but I'm afraid we don't do that on the forensic side of things."

"Ah." Janice tried not to let her disappointment show on her face. It seemed like this had all been a waste of time. Stuart wasn't telling them anything they didn't already know.

"Is there anything else?" Janice asked. "Anything that would help us figure out whose blood it is?"

"I'm afraid that's all I can tell you at this point," Stuart said. "You said the police were also analyzing a sample, right?"

Janice nodded. The police still had that knife, with the sample of dark brown powder she thought was probably also blood.

"Maybe they'll be able to come back with something more," Stuart said, though he looked doubtful.

"We really appreciate your help," Janice said.

"Yes, thank you." LuAnn took the folder from him. "It's so kind of you to help us, especially with all the other things you have going on."

Like planning a wedding, Janice thought. She stopped herself from saying it just in time.

"I'm glad to help." Stuart handed Janice the bag with the dress inside. "Let me know if you need anything else."

"We will," Janice promised. She gave him a hug and watched as he drove out of the driveway. She said a prayer for his safety, and then she turned back to LuAnn.

"It's probably about time to get ready to go see Irene," she said.

LuAnn agreed, and they both went upstairs to get ready. Not long afterward, they were pulling into the driveway of the Bickerton mansion, with its towering stone walls and leaded glass windows. They made their way up the flagstone walkway, edged with evergreen shrubs, and rang the doorbell. A few minutes later they were ushered into the library, lined in floor-to-ceiling bookcases and thick hardback books piled everywhere. Heavy velvet drapes were pulled aside to let the winter light in, but the room still had a heavy, oppressive feel.

Janice and LuAnn sat on the love seat, and Irene lowered herself, painfully slowly, into an armchair covered in ornate crewelwork.

Finally settled in her seat, she looked at them through the large blue frames of her glasses.

"So," she said, "you want to know about the buildings that used to be at the back of your property?"

"That's right," LuAnn said. "We were told that your husband Fred owned them at one time, and we were interested in anything you could tell us about them."

"They were lovely buildings," Irene said. "Solidly built, well-constructed, affordable homes with fenced-in yards for the working class."

Janice did a better job of hiding her surprise to all of this than LuAnn, who made a noise somewhere between a laugh and a choke.

"That's good to hear," Janice said as diplomatically as she could. "We had heard there were some problems with the buildings along the way. But you're saying that they didn't start out that way?" What she'd really wanted to ask was if Irene was living in an alternate reality, but she knew she had to be careful if she didn't want to offend her. Then they would never find out anything about the buildings.

"There were some issues with tenants damaging the properties," Irene said. "It was a constant struggle, really. People like that don't care for their things, which explains why they don't have much to begin with."

Janice forced herself to bite back the response that threatened to come out. They wouldn't get anywhere if they offended her, she reminded herself.

"Do you know how long your husband owned the buildings?" LuAnn asked. Her voice was just a tad too high-pitched, too strained, and Janice could see that she was fighting to keep her tone pleasant too.

"Oh, let's see. He bought them from his father around his thirty-fourth or thirty-fifth birthday, I think. His father sold them for a song, you see. It was his way of getting him into the family business. That would put it around 1960 or so."

As she was speaking, Thelma, Irene's older sister, came shuffling into the room holding a tea tray. Janice wasn't sure how she was able to balance the tray with the cane she used, but somehow, she managed to make her way into the room and set the tray down on the polished mahogany coffee table.

"Here you go," she said, gesturing at the tray. There were sugar cookies and lemon squares on a dainty china plate edged in gold. Then she sat down in the armchair across from Irene and reached for a lemon square. Janice hadn't realized she'd been planning on joining them. Judging by the look on Irene's face, she hadn't realized it either.

"So he managed the buildings from 1960 or so until... when?" Janice asked.

"Until they burned down. Terrible thing, that." Irene shifted in her chair. Janice noted that this meant Fred had definitely owned the land at the time the box had been buried. "Smoking, you know. Someone fell asleep with a lit cigarette, and the whole place went up. It was so awful."

"Especially the lawsuit," Thelma said wryly.

"Oh hush." Irene waved her hand at her sister. "Yes, it was awful how they dragged Fred to court over the carelessness of the tenants. You know Fred couldn't be held responsible for the alterations his tenants made. But that was not what I meant, and you know it." She turned to Janice and LuAnn. "A couple of people lost their lives, you see. It was just awful. Several of the apartments had walls that had been erected to divide them up so more people could fit into them. They weren't up to code and were in strange places, just chopping the apartments up into tiny bits, and people got confused and couldn't find their way out in all the smoke." She turned back to her sister. "But you know Fred was not found guilty of that. He couldn't help what the tenants had done."

"They couldn't prove he was responsible," Thelma said. "That hotshot lawyer was worth every penny."

Irene shot her sister a look, and then she leaned forward and took a sugar cookie.

"That's terrible," LuAnn said. "But they were able to determine the cause of the fire, then, and show that he couldn't have been responsible for someone smoking. That's good."

"Oh yes. It was definitely a cigarette. Or maybe a candle that was left burning."

So, not definite, then, Janice thought.

"Probably needed the candle to stay warm," Thelma said under her breath.

If Irene heard the comment, she ignored it. "Anyway, after the fire, the buildings were a total loss, and poor Fred didn't have the heart to rebuild."

"Or the money," Thelma added quietly, and again, Irene didn't seem to hear.

"He sold the land to the owner of the building that's now your inn. It was a warehouse then, of course. I think the owner planned to expand, but then the company went under, so the land just sat empty."

Janice couldn't say she was sad about that. The lawn at the back of the property was a very nice feature, and she couldn't imagine having a row of buildings on it so close to the inn.

"We were particularly interested in learning about a business called Dudley's, which was located in one of the buildings there," LuAnn said. "Do you remember the place?"

"Of course." Irene polished off the cookie, but a crumb hung to her top lip. "Dudley's was a big part of the problem with that place."

"What do you mean?" LuAnn asked, meeting Janice's eye. They'd both heard what others had said about it, but Janice was intrigued to hear Irene's take on the tavern.

"Oh, well, you know. It was probably inevitable. Having a tavern right there, near where they lived… The temptation was too much for some of them," Irene said. "Often they didn't have the money to pay their rent because they'd spent their paychecks on booze. That sort of thing. And then, well, you know. Gambling wasn't legal, but people do find a way, don't they? That sort of thing doesn't improve the quality of people who come in."

"Gambling?" LuAnn asked.

"Well, they could never prove it, but yes, that's what was rumored to be happening. Horses, mostly."

"Horses?" It took Janice a minute to catch up. Horses kept coming up in this investigation, and she couldn't yet see what the connection was. "You mean they were betting on horse racing?"

"Exactly." Irene reached for another cookie. "There's a track just across the river, you know."

Janice didn't know.

"I never did see the appeal, but apparently plenty of people did. Gambled away their rent money and more, some of them."

"This happened at Dudley's?" Janice asked.

"Not out in the open, of course," Irene said. "But I'm told it certainly did happen."

Janice didn't really know much about how gambling worked, but she knew there had to have been someone heading it all up.

"So wait, how did it work? Don't you have to be at a racetrack to bet on horse racing?" she asked.

"Yes, legally you do," Irene said. "But if someone just across the river is willing to act as an intermediary... Well, let's just say there are ways." She shrugged. "Sometimes people went to the racetrack to place their bets, but sometimes they couldn't be bothered. So much easier to do it right where they lived, apparently."

"Who acted as the intermediary?" LuAnn asked. "Someone at Dudley's?"

"One of the employees, from what I understand." Irene waved her hand dismissively.

"Do you know who it was?" Janice persisted. Maybe that person was responsible for the box.

"No idea," Irene said. "I really didn't pay any attention to what was going on at that place."

"And your husband didn't know this was going on?" Janice asked.

"Of course not," Irene said at the same time Thelma snorted. Janice and LuAnn both turned to look at Thelma.

"He might not have known the details," Thelma conceded. "But who do you think loaned them the money to pay their rent?"

"It was a service he offered to keep a roof over the heads of the families," Irene said, an edge in her voice. "What did you expect him to do, cast the children out into the street because their fathers gambled away the rent money?"

"Of course," Thelma said, her smile placating. "It was a *service*."

"Naturally he had to charge interest, Thelma. Don't you try to make Fred out like he was some kind of crook. He couldn't just *give* them the money. He had to charge interest, or how would he feed our family? Certainly it was better than *evicting* them. If you're going to sit here and disparage my husband, you can find another room to sit in."

Thelma reached for another lemon bar. "You're right. I'm sorry," she said. But she didn't look a bit sorry, Janice thought.

And Janice wasn't sorry either, because now she understood how it had all worked. Fred wasn't just the landlord. He had also made high-interest loans to those who had lost their money either drinking or gambling. And Janice couldn't say for sure, but something in her said that box they'd found was connected to one of the people tied up in this.

"Do you happen to have any records of the people he might have lent money to? Or people who lived in the buildings?"

Irene tilted her head. "Why? What is this all about, anyway?"

"You see, we found something," LuAnn started. They'd discussed on the way over here how they would explain their questions. "We had some work done on our plumbing—"

"Oh yes, because of your sewage problem," Irene said. "I heard."

She'd heard? Did everyone know about the problem with the sewage? Janice had been hoping the news hadn't spread. It sure didn't do much for an inn's reputation. But LuAnn was already moving past that before she could ask.

"Well, anyway, we found something buried in the yard, in what would likely have been directly behind Dudley's. We're trying to figure out who might have buried it and why."

"What was it?" Thelma asked.

They had worried about how much to say, conscious that whatever they told Irene and Thelma would surely end up all over town. But they had decided that there was a chance that one of them would recognize one of the objects and be able to cast new light on the discovery.

"You said there were fenced-in yards behind each of the buildings?" LuAnn asked.

"Yes. Private gardens just for the tenants and business. Really, you couldn't have asked for nicer accommodations, but did they appreciate it? No they did not."

Janice pulled out her phone and showed the photos of the objects to both Thelma and Irene, but neither of them seemed to recognize any of them.

"Looks like a collection of someone's garbage." Irene brushed the sugar off her fingertips, letting the crumbs fall to the floor. "Maybe the person thought dumping it in the yard was easier than disposing of it properly."

Janice didn't think that was likely. Why would someone lock their garbage in a metal box before burying it in the ground?

"We were thinking it might be more likely that it's evidence in a crime of some sort," LuAnn said. "We had the dress tested, and that stain is definitely blood. So we're hoping to get ahold of names of people who might have had some connection to Dudley's, or access to the yard."

"Hmm." Irene shifted again in her seat. From this angle, you could see that her white hair was starting to thin along the sides. "I don't know. I don't really have any clue where I would even look for something like that."

"What about all those boxes in the attic? Aren't there a number of them filled with files from Fred's old office?" Thelma asked. "There are several filing cabinets' worth of stuff in there. I bet you could find something."

Irene shot her sister another look. "Well," she said, "I suppose I could take a look."

"We sure would appreciate it," LuAnn said. "We would love to be able to figure this thing out."

"I'll let you know if I find anything," Irene said. LuAnn and Janice thanked her, and after a few more minutes of conversation, they started for home.

"That was interesting," LuAnn said as they climbed into the car. "Forget the family business. It seems Fred's real business was usury."

"It does seem like he took advantage of people down on their luck," Janice agreed. "What a nasty business."

"But does it mean he got tied up in all this?" LuAnn asked. "I don't think it necessarily does."

"No, certainly not," Janice said. "But what do you make of Irene's hesitation to look through Fred's old files?"

"If they're in the attic, she might not want to climb the steps. And it does sound like a chore."

"Frankly, I'm surprised to hear there are still files in his office. He must have passed away, what, at least a decade ago?" After a moment, Janice added, "Cynthia said the same thing about her father's files. Don't people deal with their things?"

"I think a lot of people find it difficult," LuAnn said. She'd started going through her mother's things last year, and she'd found it harder than she'd expected to decide what to do with some of the things her mother had loved. She was still trying to figure out what she was supposed to do with her mother's old keepsakes and trying to make sense of what paperwork she was required to hold on to for legal purposes. "And Irene isn't young."

"I suppose you're right." Janice hadn't enjoyed going through Lawrence's things when he'd passed away, but she'd known it had to be done. But she supposed not everyone was in the same boat she was in. "Well, it will be interesting to see what she turns up."

"If she turns anything up," LuAnn pointed out. "And even if she does find something, will she turn it over to us?"

"I suppose all we can do is wait and see," Janice said.

That was the problem, though, Janice thought. It felt like all they were doing was waiting. And waiting wasn't getting them any closer to finding out what had really happened.

The sun set early this time of year, and dusk had already gathered on the horizon by five o'clock. Janice tried not to let the gloom get to her, but it was hard, especially as the gathering shadows matched her dark mood. She'd tried calling Stacy twice, but she hadn't picked up either time. Now, Janice was gazing out through the fourth-floor windows, staring at the lights that had started to twinkle on the far side of the river. There were plenty of things she should be doing here. Several angles she could be looking into to help get to the bottom of the mystery. But she couldn't focus on anything at the moment. She needed to talk to Stacy. She'd thought about what Stuart had said, what Tess had said. And she'd spent a long time in prayer this afternoon asking God to make it clear whether she was in the wrong. She realized she was. She needed to make it right.

Finally, Janice made a decision.

"I'm going out for a bit," she called to Tess, who was busy with something in her bedroom.

"Be home by curfew," Tess called. Janice shook her head. Tess had to make a joke out of everything. Usually Janice found this habit amusing, but today, when she was already on edge, she wasn't in the mood to laugh.

"I'm going to try to talk to Stacy," Janice said.

"In that case, I'll be praying."

Janice thanked her and headed downstairs. Her shoulders tightened up as she drove toward Stacy's, and when she pulled into the driveway, she forced herself to take several long breaths. *Please Lord, help me to be humble, and give me the words to make it right.*

Finally, she got out of the car, and, pulling her scarf up over her nose against the bitter wind, she climbed the stairs and knocked on Stacy's door. She could hear the high-pitched whistling that meant the TV was on inside. Janice had a brief moment of panic—what if Dash was here? She hadn't thought about that. What if he was actually living here? But when Stacy pulled the door open, Janice didn't see any sign of him. Larry was sitting on the couch watching cartoons.

Stacy let out a sigh when she saw her mother. "Hi."

"Hi." Janice held out the cookies she'd brought. "I wanted to apologize."

Stacy hesitated, and then gestured for Janice to step inside.

"Thank you for inviting me over on Thursday," Janice said. She still held the plate of cookies awkwardly in front of her, but Stacy made no move to take them. Larry hadn't even looked up from the television. "Thank you for introducing me to Dash. I understand that he is a big part of your life, and I want to get to know him."

"Really?" Stacy cocked her head. She reminded Janice of Lawrence's mother when she did that. "Because you didn't really seem all that interested in getting to know him last week. Mostly you seemed to be interested in making him feel bad because he didn't meet your high standards."

"I know," Janice said. "I didn't mean to communicate that, but I can see now that I did. And that's why I need to apologize."

She could see Stacy's resolve start to waver. Janice pressed on.

"I see now that I acted badly. I had a vision in my head for the kind of person I would pick out for you. And I let that influence my behavior."

"You didn't even give him a chance. You saw the way he looks and what his job is, and you decided he wasn't good enough."

"You're right." Janice hated that it was true, but it was.

"The thing is, Mom, I think if you got to know him, you'd find that he's actually a really great guy. The kind of person you always told me to look for—someone who treats me well and respects me and lets his faith guide him."

"His faith?"

"Yes, Mom." Stacy rolled her eyes. "Dash is a Christian. He even took some classes at a seminary years ago, thinking he might become a pastor. But you didn't even give him the chance to tell you that."

Janice felt her cheeks burning as she realized that Stacy was right.

"I'm sorry." It was inadequate, she knew that, but she didn't know what else to say. "I messed up."

Stacy took in a deep breath and let it out slowly. Then, without a word, she reached out and took the plate of cookies.

"I'd like to get to know him," Janice said.

Stacy set the cookies on the table, pressed her lips together, and nodded. "Let me talk to him," she said.

Janice could see how much she'd hurt her daughter and prayed she hadn't messed things up with her for good. If Stacy felt forced to choose, Janice wasn't at all sure she would come out on top.

"I'll give you a call."

For now, it would have to do.

LuAnn was reading on the couch when Janice came up to the fourth floor. She heard Tess on the phone in her bedroom. A pot was simmering on the stove, and it smelled delicious.

"How did it go?" LuAnn placed her bookmark in her book and closed it. "Tess told me where you were going."

"It was all right," Janice said. "Probably about as well as could be expected, considering."

"I'm glad to hear it." LuAnn patted the space next to her on the couch. Tom perched on the back of the couch. "There's hot water in the kettle if you want tea. And I'm making a white bean stew for dinner."

"That sounds wonderful," Janice said. She prepared a cup of mint tea, and then she sat down next to LuAnn.

"Do you want to talk about it?" LuAnn asked.

Janice blew on the tea, causing ripples to spread across the surface. Warm steam brushed her face. She wasn't sure she wanted to revisit the conversation so soon—or ever.

"I don't think so," she said. "But thank you."

"I understand," LuAnn said. "Do you want to hear some good news?"

"Yes, please. Anything positive would be welcome."

"I got a call from Cynthia Cook."

"Really?" Janice took a sip of the tea. It was still too hot and burned her tongue.

"She said she had gone through the boxes in the basement and found a few things relating to Dudley's. She was going to be home tomorrow and asked if we wanted to come by to take a look."

"What kind of things?"

"She didn't say." LuAnn took a sip of tea. "So. Do you want to take a trip to Cincinnati tomorrow?"

Janice smiled. "You better believe it."

CHAPTER TEN

May 20, 1861

Anna had gotten worse since the doctor had come the day before. She seemed weaker now, and though her fever had come down a bit, the rash was still spreading over her body. The broth Prudence had tried to get her to drink was cooling on the bedside table.

"'Yea, though I walk through the valley of the shadow of death, I will fear no evil, for thou art with me.'" Prudence had been reading from the Psalms for the last hour or so. They didn't seem to bring Anna much comfort, but they filled Prudence with peace. "'Thy rod and thy staff, they comfort me.'"

"Did thee find it?" Anna said, though her speech was so slurred she had to repeat it before Prudence could make sense of her words.

"The box? Not yet," Prudence said.

"Need...find it," Anna managed to say. "Important things..."

"Yes," Prudence said. She brushed away the hair that was plastered to Anna's forehead. "I have looked for it, but I have not found it."

"Please..." Anna said. "Find it."

Prudence waited for her to say more, maybe give her even a hint about where to look. But she didn't say anything more. Prudence turned back to her Bible and started reading again. "'Thou preparest a table before me in the presence of mine enemies: thou anointest my head with oil; my cup runneth over.'"

Prudence continued to read until Anna once again fell into an uneasy sleep. Then she stood and stepped forward to take the bowl of broth. As she did, her foot kicked against something under the bed. Prudence bent down and looked under the bed, and she gasped.

Could it really be? She reached for the metal box and slid it out from under the bed. Could this be what she'd been looking for all along?

Monday morning, after they'd cleaned up from breakfast and made sure Robin and Taylor were coming in, LuAnn and Janice set off for Cincinnati. Tess had offered to stay home and keep the inn running. It would take over three hours to get to the address Cynthia had given them, so they started out early. LuAnn had offered to drive, which left Janice free to relax in the passenger seat. The day was clear and dry, though cold, and for a while they listened to worship music as the miles began to disappear.

As they merged onto the main highway, LuAnn spoke up. "I couldn't sleep last night."

"Oh dear. Do you want me to take over the driving?" Janice asked.

"No, thank you. I'm fine." LuAnn pulled the wand on the steering wheel and cleaned the windshield. "I couldn't sleep because I was thinking."

"About what?"

"Horses."

Janice turned toward her. "They do keep coming up in this investigation, don't they?"

"They do. At first, I thought the connection to Bronwyn and her friend Marilyn was the most obvious. They spent time at the stables and rode horses and such."

"Growing up riding horses sounds pretty great, doesn't it?" Janice said. "What little girl doesn't want a pony?"

"I never quite saw the appeal, to be honest," LuAnn said. "I wanted a puppy."

"Much easier to clean up after."

"I never did get one, though. Not on the salary my mom made at the diner," LuAnn said. "Oh well. At least we have Huck now."

"Huck is pretty great," Janice said. "But he won't solve this mystery for us. Tell me more about the horses."

"Well, in addition to the Marilyn and Bronwyn connection, there was that article in the page of newspaper we found in the box."

"Right," Janice said. "It was about the new up and coming jockey at Hillsborough Racetrack, but it mentioned the stable where Bronwyn and her friends kept their horses. It's connected to the racetrack."

"Right. The one that Irene mentioned yesterday," LuAnn said. "So last night, I did some research into the racetrack."

"What did you find?" Janice asked.

"It closed down in the 1980s."

"I can't say I'm sad to hear that. Doesn't it sound barbaric, whipping horses to run around in circles? Gambling money away over the winner?"

"I don't know. Have you ever seen a horse running? It's a beautiful sight. They're so powerful and graceful, all at once."

"I guess." Janice still wasn't sure about the rest of it though.

"Well, anyway, the racetrack closed because mismanagement led to a big financial issue. But for decades, it did really well. Betting on horses was one of the few official ways to gamble in West Virginia until fairly recently."

"And as we now know, it wasn't only legal betting that was happening in association with the racetrack," Janice said.

"That's right," LuAnn said. "Bets were being placed not just at the racetrack itself, which is the only place where it's legal, but in Dudley's, if Irene is to be believed. On the Ohio side of the river, which made it doubly illegal."

"Can something be doubly illegal?"

"I have no idea," LuAnn admitted. "But in any case, I don't know why Irene would make that up."

"So it's possible that gambling had something to do with how blood ended up on that knife and the dress."

"I think it is definitely possible," Janice said. She picked up the tumbler of coffee she had set in the cup holder and took a sip. "But I still don't see the connection. How would Marilyn or Peggy or Lidia have anything to do with gambling?"

"See, that's where I really went down the rabbit hole," LuAnn said. "I asked myself the same question, and then I looked back through all the information I could find. Something was bothering me—something had caught in my brain, and I couldn't quite unearth what it was."

"Did you figure it out?"

"Yes, but only after I looked back through the copy of the police file for Lidia Jankowski."

Janice took another sip and held the warm metal thermos between her hands. "What did you find?"

"I was reading back through the pages of interviews and I saw that Jacob Opalinski, who only grudgingly sent Lidia's mom child support money some months, had an interesting job."

"What was that?"

"He was a farrier."

Janice searched her brain. "And…they do what exactly?"

"They trim horse's hooves."

"Ah." Janice was beginning to see the connection. "So he could have spent time at the stables or racetrack."

"He no doubt did."

"But I thought he had a solid alibi for the night Lidia was killed."

"He did."

Janice didn't see where LuAnn was going with any of this. "Okay, so what's the connection?"

"It was really buried, but in his testimony, Jacob Opalinski mentioned that part of the reason his wife was getting upset was because Lidia had been contacting members of his family, wanting to connect."

"The wife knew about Lidia all along, right?"

"Yes, but I imagine there's a big difference between knowing your husband cheated on you and fathered a child and having that child reach out and want to become friendly with your own children."

Janice could see that. But she could also see the other side. "But surely Lidia had a right to know her half-siblings."

"Maybe. You would think so. But apparently Martina Opalinski didn't think so."

"Okay…." Janice still didn't see it. "So, Lidia wanted to get to know her half-siblings. Their mom didn't want that to happen. Are you suggesting that Martina Opalinski lured her down under the Harmar Bridge and stabbed her?"

"No. Though that's an interesting theory I hadn't thought of. I'll add that to the list," LuAnn said.

"Oh dear."

"What I was thinking was, wouldn't it be useful to know the names of Jacob Opalinski's children? They aren't mentioned anywhere in the file. Why is that?"

"Probably because it's not relevant." Janice shrugged. "Or at least the police didn't think it was."

"Exactly. The police didn't think it was. But that doesn't mean they didn't miss something. We've already discussed how they didn't do a great job on the case."

"True." But Janice was still skeptical.

"Well, I called the History and Genealogy Archive this morning as soon as they opened."

"How did you do that?" They'd left the inn shortly after ten.

"I called a few minutes before ten. I knew that Danny always gets there early."

"How did you know that?"

"I *like* history," LuAnn said. "And I talk to people."

"Okay," Janice said. She could admit that LuAnn was more likely to engage in small talk and find out tidbits like this.

"So, did Danny help you find Jacob's family tree?"

"It wasn't all that hard, really. How many Opalinskis have you ever met?"

"I'm pretty sure I couldn't spell it if you paid me."

"He had two sons and a daughter with Martina Opalinski," LuAnn said. "Joanna, Oskar, and Sebastian. And Danny was kind enough to run the names through their systems to see if they returned any results."

"And?"

"It turns out all veterinarian licenses granted in the state are public record."

"Okay...."

"Oskar Opalinski was twenty-five when he was granted his veterinary license in the state of Ohio. His specialty, obviously, was horses. Guess where he got a job?"

"Oh, don't say it's—"

"That's right. Hillsborough Racetrack. Working with the horses there."

Janice thought this through, trying to fit this new information into the holes they had. Lidia's name started with *L*; her mom was far away and Lidia might not have had an address to send her letters; her father had been at Dudley's the night she died. But aside from a half brother she didn't know who worked at Hillsborough Racetrack, there wasn't any clear connection to horses. And they didn't know if the dress or the bracelet or the knife were connected to her. "That doesn't necessarily mean that he had anything to do with Lidia," she said.

"It doesn't," LuAnn agreed. "But it does seem that the police didn't do as thorough a job as they should have on Lidia's case."

"I suppose they did the best they could," Janice said. She thought through what LuAnn had said. "So your theory is that Oskar Opalinski was contacted by his half sister, agreed to meet up with her one night, and killed her?"

"It's just a theory."

"Why would he do that?"

"Why do people do stupid things at all? Because they're scared or angry or jealous or greedy or sometimes for reasons that make no sense." LuAnn shrugged. "Maybe it's because Lidia's appearance was causing problems in his parents' marriage. People have killed for less reason than to keep a family intact."

"Killing your sister seems a strange way to do that."

"I'm not saying I agree. I'm not even saying I'm right. I'm just saying that it's a possible explanation." LuAnn flicked on her blinker and pulled into the left lane. "I don't think you and I are going to solve the death of Lidia Jankowski, at least not with the information we have so far. I'm just saying that we've both noticed that horses and horse racing have come up a lot in the past few days, and Lidia's brother—her much older, stronger brother—was an equine veterinarian. I think that's worth noting."

"Okay," Janice said. "I can see your point, though it's mostly conjecture at this stage."

"I'll just add one other thing," LuAnn said.

"What's that?"

"Scalpel."

"Huh?"

"Oskar was a veterinarian. They use scalpels. Lidia was stabbed with a short knife."

"Surgeons also use scalpels. Should they arrest every doctor in town? Or every postal worker? It could have been a box cutter." Janice took another sip of her coffee, and LuAnn flipped her blinker back on and moved into the middle lane just ahead of a minivan with an American flag tied to its antenna. "Besides, now you're suggesting that it wasn't the knife in the box that caused her death?"

"It was just an idea."

Janice was just getting more and more confused the longer this conversation went on.

"Let's hope that whatever records Cynthia found about Dudley's, it helps us make sense of all of this," Janice said.

"I just hope it's worth this drive," LuAnn said.

Janice laughed. "It's better than doing laundry."

"That's true," LuAnn said. "Good old Tess. I hope she's doing all right."

"I think she secretly enjoys laundry," Janice said. "Sometimes when I go into the laundry room I find her just sniffing the clean towels."

"There is something nice about the way clean towels smell," LuAnn said. She took a gulp of coffee, and they lapsed into silence. The music still played low in the background, but Janice didn't really notice it. Mostly, she tried to think through what they knew and what they suspected and how it all fit together.

Peggy O'Neal's kidnapping had never been solved, and the case files were sealed. The story had dropped from the papers. She had no known connection to the tavern or to horses or to gambling or to the word *corona*. The bracelet didn't seem likely to be hers either—she'd likely have something made of sterling, with more valuable stones. And why would she have written letters to her mom when her mom was right there in the next room? But the dress could have been hers—at least, it was about the right size, and she was the kind of wealthy teenager who wore dresses by this designer—and her initials were M.O. It was possible. What had ever happened to Peggy's parents, Janice wondered. Had they stayed in town? She had no idea. That was something she needed to look into.

There was Marilyn Oshmann. Margaret Ashworth had suspected that she'd left town when she'd turned up pregnant, but was there a more sinister reason she'd vanished? They needed to talk to Bronwyn. They'd called her again last night but hadn't gotten through. Marilyn rode horses at the stables near the racetrack, and Margaret said that she and Bronwyn had worn dresses like the one they'd found, and she had the right initials. But was that enough to tie her to the box?

Then there was Lidia Jankowski. In some ways, she seemed the most plausible connection. But in other ways, it still didn't seem to fit. It was like they had all these puzzle pieces and kept trying to force them into the open spots, and none of them fit just right.

Janice couldn't help feeling that they hadn't found the right piece yet. That there was still a clue out there that would make this whole thing suddenly make more sense. What were they missing?

She thought back over the past few days, thinking through all the strange things that had happened since the workers had unearthed that box in the yard. And she remembered something.

"LuAnn," she said. How could she phrase this exactly?

"Yep?"

"The other night, when Brad came over..."

"Yes?"

"Did he mention anything about any of the objects in the box?"

"What?" LuAnn's brow wrinkled. "No. Why would he?"

"I don't know," Janice said. "Except that when he came into the inn, he saw them all spread out, and... I could have been misreading it, but I would have sworn he saw something he recognized."

"Which object was it?" LuAnn asked.

Janice shook her head. "I don't know. He just looked over at the table and... Well, it was hard to tell exactly. But the look on his face... It was like he'd seen one of the items before."

"If that's true, why wouldn't he say so?"

"I don't know," Janice said. "And maybe I misread the look on his face...."

But Janice knew she hadn't.

"That must be it," LuAnn said. "I'm sure he would have said something if he'd recognized anything that was in that box."

"Yeah," Janice said. "But would you mind asking him, just to be sure?"

LuAnn shrugged again. "Okay," she said. "I'll call him later and ask him." But the tone of her voice made it clear she didn't think there was any way he could be involved.

And maybe he wasn't, Janice thought. But still. It didn't hurt to find out.

Cynthia lived in a beautiful Tudor-style home in a neighborhood filled with shops and restaurants. The streets were lined with well-built houses, and trees, now bare in the winter light, arched over the roads. Janice imagined it must be beautiful in the summer.

They parked in the narrow driveway and made their way up the cement walkway. The doorbell echoed inside, and then Cynthia opened the door.

"Hello," she said, pulling the door open to usher them inside. "Come on in."

"Thank you," LuAnn said.

"This is lovely." Janice looked around, taking in the bright and airy living room, the dining area with a long wooden table, and the open kitchen with shaker gray cabinets and a large marble island. The house was very traditional on the outside but had a modern, warm feel on the inside.

"Thank you," Cynthia said. "When we bought this house, nothing had been changed in several decades. There was still shag carpeting and vinyl paneling in the living room." She laughed. "So we basically gutted it and started over."

"You did a great job," LuAnn said.

"Anyway, thank you for coming all this way," Cynthia said. "I'm sorry to ask you to do so, but I wasn't going to be able to make it back to Marietta for a few weeks."

"You didn't make us," LuAnn said. "You offered to mail the files. I just didn't want to wait."

Wait, what? Janice turned to LuAnn, who gave her a guilty smile.

"I hope what I found is worth the drive," Cynthia said. "I'm not sure it's of any value, but I did find some files in my parents' boxes that mentioned Dudley's." She indicated a stack of file folders on the credenza by the door.

"We're grateful you took the time to search," Janice said.

"It was kind of fun, to be honest. And it was long past time to sort through all that stuff anyway. Most of it was just junk I hadn't dealt with. But I found some family photos and lots of things I didn't know existed."

"I am in the process of sorting through my mother's things," LuAnn said. "It's hard, because everything I find reminds me of her. But it's great, because everything I find reminds me of her."

Somehow LuAnn always knew the right thing to say. Janice wished she had that skill.

"Exactly." Cynthia smiled at LuAnn. "Well, anyway, I hope you find what you're looking for here, and I'm sorry I wasn't able to be more help."

"You've been a big help," Janice said. "And we're grateful."

After a stop at a famous chili restaurant for lunch—for some reason this chili had spaghetti in it, which Janice thought was odd but tasty—they were back on the road and headed home. Janice had offered to drive this leg of the journey, and LuAnn had glanced through the folders Cynthia had given them, but she didn't find anything that stood out to her as an obvious clue, and eventually she dozed off in the passenger seat while Janice drove. Praise music played softly in the background, but Janice was occupied thinking through everything they'd learned in the past few days, looking at bits of information from different angles, trying to make sense of it.

They were only about a half hour from home when LuAnn's phone rang, and she startled awake and dug through her purse to pull it out.

"Hi, Brad," LuAnn said.

Janice only heard LuAnn's end of the conversation, but she pieced together the fact that his aunt Irene had found something relating to the old buildings on their property and asked him to deliver it to LuAnn. Goodness. Old files, twice in one day. Whatever Irene had found had to be over fifty years old. Hadn't these people ever heard of Marie Kondo? LuAnn told him they would be home later that afternoon and suggested he come over on his way home from work.

After LuAnn hung up, Janice asked a question that had been floating around in her mind for the past fifty miles.

"How would you feel about making a stop on the way home?"

"Where were you thinking?"

"How about a stop at the Hillsborough Racetrack?"

LuAnn gave her a sly smile. "I love it. I just wish I'd thought of it."

Even though the racetrack had been closed for decades, it wasn't hard to find. Weeds sprouted up between the cracks in the cement that had once been a parking lot. Paint was peeling from the tall edifice at the front, but you could still make out the words HILLSBOROUGH RACETRACK. They walked up to the first of a half-dozen gates that had once served as an entrance, but it was locked. Janice tried each of them, while LuAnn went off searching for another way in.

Janice wasn't sure what they were looking for, exactly. But after thinking through the clues they had for most of the way back, she was even more convinced that horses, or horse racing, was tied up in this all somehow.

"Over here!" LuAnn called. Janice had to walk around the curved end of the building before she found LuAnn pushing open what looked like a door that had once been a service entrance at the side of the track. It opened smoothly when LuAnn pulled the handle. "We're clearly not the first people to come in here," she said, indicating the smashed locking mechanism.

"Do you think it's okay for us to be in here?" Janice asked. They were probably technically trespassing, though she had no idea who owned the property these days.

"We're not going to do anything. Just take a look around," LuAnn said. She hadn't exactly answered the question, but before she could talk herself out of it, Janice followed her through the door. They walked down a short hallway to the back of what had apparently once been a concession stand, judging by the metal counter and the ghost lettering on the sign behind it. Most of the white plastic letters had long ago fallen out of the grooved felt background, but the sunlight had bleached the fabric enough to leave the images of the letters behind.

"A hot dog was only fifty cents," Janice noticed.

"What a deal."

A metal roll-top gate was pulled down and bolted to the counter, but there was a door next to it that was hanging from its hinges. LuAnn pushed it open easily, and then they were in the main concourse. High above them, the concrete roof held the next level of seats in the grandstand, and counters behind glass, like ticket windows at an old train station, with the words BETTING STATION over them were spread around the main level. Signs above the stations must have once displayed the lineup of each race, Janice realized. In front of them, cracked plastic seats sloped down toward the racetrack. Both the dirt track and the infield were now overgrown with weeds, and on the far side was a high fence. Enough boards in the fence had broken that they could see what looked like a block of stables behind and several outbuildings past that. Broken bottles newspapers, and trash were scattered all around them.

"We're definitely not the first people to be in here," LuAnn said, kicking at a crushed can. A liquid leaked out a hole in the side.

Janice agreed as a gust of wind blew in from the field and under the awning. It was dark and cold under here, but she imagined it must have been nice and cool on a hot summer day. She tried to imagine what it had been like here, once upon a time, with the seats full of spectators and the powerful horses zooming around the track, the jockeys in their colorful outfits bobbing up and down on their backs. Now that she was here she could see that it must have been pretty impressive. True, the gambling aspect of it didn't appeal to her. And it was possible that her vision had been influenced by images she'd seen of the Kentucky Derby, because in the vision in her imagination, all the women were wearing pastel dresses and elaborate hats. Most likely this racetrack had never attracted that sort of crowd, she realized. But still. LuAnn was right. Horses were so powerful and so beautiful. Watching them race like that… It must have been something.

"Janice," LuAnn said, coming up beside her. "Look."

Janice followed LuAnn's finger, which was pointing at a series of horses painted on the walls in between the betting windows. Just behind them, another horse was painted on the wall, this time a black horse with a silky dark mane. Underneath the horse were the words FLYING EBONY, and beneath that were the years 1945, 1947, and 1948. Just down the concourse was a picture of a gray horse, and MOONSHINE was written underneath, along with 1951 and 1952. Those must have been the horses' names, she realized, and probably years they'd won a big race of some sort. Down at the far end, she could see paintings of Dakota, who'd been a champion in the late seventies, and Gunpowder, from the early seventies. And there, listed as a champion in the early 1960s, was a picture of a gorgeous sleek bay horse. Janice gasped. A beautiful sleek bay horse named Corona.

"I think we might have just found the connection we were looking for," LuAnn said, her eyes wide.

CHAPTER ELEVEN

When LuAnn and Janice got back to the inn in the late afternoon, they found Tess hunched over LuAnn's thesaurus, which was open to the *C*'s. A notebook was spread out next to her, and she had a pencil in her hand.

"If you're looking up the word *corona* again, you can stop right now," Janice said, and they explained about their trip to the racetrack.

"Now you tell me," Tess said, and closed the heavy book. "A horse?" She cocked her head. "So what does the horse have to do with all this?"

"We don't know that yet," LuAnn said. "But at least it's a new direction."

"True." Tess tapped the eraser of her pencil on the thesaurus. "What else did you find?"

"Cynthia gave us these folders." LuAnn placed the manila file folders on the table. "I glanced through them and didn't see anything that jumped out at me, but we'll need to look through it all more carefully." She lowered herself into the chair across from Janice. "What have you been up to today?"

"Oh, you know. Mostly eating bonbons and such," Tess said.

"Right." Janice nodded. "That sounds likely."

Tess laughed. "Actually, aside from, you know, running our entire business on my own, I learned a few things myself."

"Like what?"

"I kept wondering about how and why the Peggy O'Neal case file was sealed, and why the story dropped from the papers if it was as big a story as you remember it, Janice."

"I've been wondering that too," Janice said, and LuAnn nodded.

"So I called my sister-in-law Carrie. She's an attorney. She practices mostly family law, but I figured it was worth a shot."

"What did she say?"

"She said it sounded like the family had filed an injunction."

"A what?" Janice had heard the word, but she didn't know what it meant.

"The way Carrie explained it, an injunction is basically when the court orders you to do something, or stop doing something," Tess said.

"Like stop printing news about a story in the newspaper?" LuAnn asked, her eyes wide.

"Exactly." Tess nodded. "Or to seal up a police case file."

"But…" Janice tried to make sense of this. "Is that possible? How is that legal?"

"Carrie couldn't say without more information. Obviously she doesn't know the specifics of the case. But that was her best guess about what happened based on what I told her," Tess said.

"But how would someone even go about doing that?" LuAnn asked.

"Carrie said that a lawyer would file a motion, and a judge would grant the injunction, or not."

"And it appears that they did in this case," Janice said. "Which must mean there's something really important in that file."

"Or something really embarrassing," Tess said darkly. "Something the family didn't want to get out."

"But surely a judge wouldn't grant the request unless there was a good reason, right?" LuAnn asked. "What could be important enough that he would grant such a request?"

"The other alternative is that the request could have come from someone with a lot of power," Tess said.

"You mean a powerful lawyer," Janice said.

"She means a powerful *father*," LuAnn clarified. "Peggy's father was the president of the bank at the time, right?"

"Oh. Right." Now Janice saw what she was getting at. "So for some reason, Peggy's father wanted the story shut down and the files sealed, and he was powerful enough to make it happen."

"That was Carrie's guess," Tess said.

"If she's right—and it seems to make perfect sense if she is—the natural question is why," LuAnn said. "What was in the file that he didn't want to get out?"

"I'd sure love to find that out," Tess said.

"So how do we do that?" Janice asked. "Did Carrie have any suggestions for that?"

"I'm afraid not," Tess said. "So I did the obvious thing."

Janice and LuAnn both looked at her, waiting for her to explain. With Tess, the obvious thing could really be anything.

"I looked in the phone book," Tess said, narrowing her eyes. "What did you guys think I meant?"

"Ordered a pizza was my first guess," Janice admitted.

"I assumed you watched cat videos on YouTube," LuAnn said.

"You guys." She shook her head. "What in the world? What must you think of me?"

LuAnn and Janice shrugged.

"*Anyway*," Tess said. "I did the obvious thing and looked to see if any of the family still lived in the area. I had the father's name from these articles"—she pointed to the printouts of the articles Janice had brought home—"and there was no listing for a Douglas O'Neal. What I found for him was an obituary from a newspaper in Arizona, and one from his wife a few years ago."

"So they're definitely not available to answer questions for us."

"Correct." Tess nodded. "I also looked for info for the neighbor who saw the car idling outside the house, and I had that name too, Paul LeBreux. But Paul apparently passed away many years ago."

"It sounds like that was a dead end," Janice said.

"It could have been, except that I noticed there were two O'Neal families listed. I called them both, and one of them was a relative. He is Douglas's nephew. Peggy's cousin."

"And what did he say?" LuAnn asked.

"He was really weird once I mentioned I was interested in finding out what happened to Peggy."

"Really weird how?" Janice asked.

"Like, stumbling all over his words. He wasn't sure what to say. But he finally told me that I would have to talk to Sam."

"Who's Sam?" LuAnn asked.

But Janice remembered reading his name in the articles about the kidnapping. "That's Peggy's younger brother."

Janice couldn't believe she hadn't thought of it sooner. How had she forgotten that Peggy had a younger brother? "Did he give you a number for Sam?"

"No. But he told me that he teaches at Stanford. It wasn't hard to find a number for him after that. So I called and left a message. Hopefully he'll call back."

"Wow. You have had a productive day."

"Oh, and we got a call back from Bronwyn Meyers. Previously Bronwyn Ashworth. She said she had to check in on her aunt tonight and could stop by this evening to talk to us."

"It's funny to think of someone checking in on Margaret," LuAnn said. "She seems so fierce."

"She is that," Tess said. "But she's also got to be in her eighties."

"That's true," Janice said.

"Well, I'm glad she's coming by," LuAnn said. "And Brad is also coming by later to drop off something his aunt Irene found."

"Sounds like it's going to be a busy evening," Tess said.

"Why don't I go ahead and get dinner started?" LuAnn suggested.

Janice was still stuffed from lunch, but she was glad that LuAnn would take the lead on dinner. "Why don't I take a look through the files that Cynthia gave us?"

"Sounds good," said Tess. She picked up the thesaurus and started to carry it to LuAnn's room.

Janice opened up the top file folder, labeled DUDLEY'S on the tab, and saw that it was full of invoices from liquor distributors, glassware manufacturers, and food services companies. Janice looked through each one carefully, but she didn't see anything that seemed to be a clue.

The second file folder contained employee records, a few pay stubs, and a list of unpaid tabs. It was good to have a list of names, Janice supposed. But she wasn't sure what to do with it. Who were these people, and what did any of them have to do with how that box ended up in the backyard?

The last file folder made even less sense. It held loose notebook papers with illegible notes on them, and napkins with random phone numbers, and pen and ink drawings stained by brown liquid. After she'd looked through each one carefully, Janice let out a sigh and closed the folder. She stretched her arms up over her head.

"Did you find anything?" LuAnn called. She was slicing raw chicken into thin strips.

"No." Janice hated to admit it. She hadn't been sure what the files might contain, but she'd hoped it would be more interesting than this. "I'm afraid we might have driven seven hours today for no good reason."

"That chili was a good reason," LuAnn said.

"It was good, but I don't know if I'd go that far," Janice said.

"I'm trying to be positive here."

"The only thing I can think of that might be of some use is these employee records."

"Do you think you might be able to track some of them down?"

"I don't know if any of them are even still alive." Janice shrugged. "But I guess it's worth a shot. Maybe some of them still worked there after Roger Morris took over the tavern and were still there in June of 1964."

She copied down the names of the fifteen or so employees mentioned in the records folder, along with the addresses listed. The smell of garlic and onions filled the space, and Janice's stomach grumbled. While LuAnn continued to work on dinner, Janice pulled out the phone book and started looking for each name. She found a few of the names with local addresses, and she copied down the numbers.

Then, a few minutes after six, the doorbell rang.

"That's got to be Brad," LuAnn said. She turned off the burner under the pan and headed for the elevator. "Is it all right with you if I see if he wants to stay for dinner?"

"That's fine with me. And I'm sure Tess won't mind."

Tess had vanished downstairs to finish up the loads of laundry she hadn't quite finished that afternoon. Janice set an extra place at the table and poured Brad a glass of water, and then she got out some crackers and that creamy goat cheese she knew Brad liked. But when the elevator dinged a moment later, just LuAnn stepped out clutching a large yellow envelope to her chest.

"No Brad?"

LuAnn shook her head. "He said he had some paperwork he had to finish up before a closing tomorrow."

"I'm sorry." She could see that LuAnn was disappointed, and to be honest, so was Janice. She'd wanted to ask him about that strange moment the other day when she'd been sure he'd recognized one of the objects from the box. Brad was a bachelor and didn't often turn down home-cooked meals. Was there any chance he was avoiding them?

It sounded silly even as she thought it. Still, though, she couldn't dismiss the thought entirely.

"That's okay," LuAnn said, but her voice was a bit too cheerful. She was disappointed, naturally. She set the envelope down on the counter, turned the burner back on, and, a moment later, tossed in the chicken. It sizzled against the hot pan. "It was nice of him to bring this by."

"I hope it proves to be more useful than the folders we got from Cynthia," Janice said.

"I hope so too."

Janice cleaned up the place she'd set for Brad, and when Tess came back upstairs, they sat down to eat the chicken fajitas LuAnn had made. The fresh cilantro and lime juice she'd sprinkled on top tasted fresh and vibrant on this dreary winter day, and they chatted about a story Tess had heard on the radio about a dog rescue center that was having trouble paying its bills and about a storm that the forecasters predicted was shaping up to blanket the Midwest under nearly a foot of snow later in the week.

They had just finished cleaning up after the meal when the doorbell rang again.

"That must be Bronwyn," Tess said, and they all hurried down the stairs to greet her at the door. Janice had tucked the metal box under her arm so she could show Bronwyn the contents.

"Hello," Janice said, pulling open the door. She'd met Bronwyn a few times when she was younger and always found her pleasant and cheerful. Her hair was a shade of brown too even to not have come from a bottle, and it was pulled up into a messy topknot. She wore a flowered tunic top over leggings and rings on most of her fingers. Tess and LuAnn introduced themselves, and Bronwyn looked around the lobby of the inn.

"Wow. Aunt Margaret told me you ladies had done this place up really nicely, but this is just gorgeous." Bronwyn had a bit of a Southern accent, which struck Janice as strange because Margaret had nothing of the sort. Could living just across the river in West Virginia be enough for her to pick up that lilting twang to her speech? "Is that a Hitchcock?" She pointed to the wooden spindle-back chair in the corner of the room.

"A reproduction," Tess said. "But yes."

"I love those chairs," Bronwyn said. "And that mantel. Was that here?"

"We had to have the wood restored, but yes, it was here when we bought the building," Janice said.

"It's really beautiful. You ladies have done such a nice job," she said, taking in the antique furniture, the bookshelves, and the tufted settee. "My aunt is not-so-secretly totally jealous that you get to live here. She's had her eye on this building since I was a kid."

As Janice recalled, Margaret was actually one of the people who had tried to stop them from buying the building and turning it into an inn. But she seemed to have come around, and Bronwyn's comment helped explain at least some of her motivation.

"Anyway, look at me, just chattering away." She turned back to the innkeepers. "Now, I have to admit that my aunt wasn't really clear about exactly what you all wanted to know. She said it was some questions about Marilyn Oshmann?"

LuAnn suggested they all sit down, and Tess and Janice settled on the settee while LuAnn and Bronwyn sat in side chairs.

"That's right," Janice said. "This is actually kind of a strange question, really. But we found this dress—"

Tess reached into the box, which Janice had set on the coffee table in front of them, and pulled out the dress and unwrapped the tissue paper. Bronwyn gasped when she saw it.

"Your aunt said it reminded her of the kinds of dresses you and your friends wore when you were teenagers—" LuAnn started.

"Oh my." Bronwyn reached out and touched the fabric gently. "Wow. This brings back memories."

"So you recognize the dress?" LuAnn asked.

"I mean, I don't know if I recognize the exact dress, but it sure looks like one Marilyn had. I was so jealous of it. I had a bunch of Lilly Pulitzers—I was kind of obsessed there for a while—but I thought she had the most gorgeous one. And it fit her perfectly too. I was always a little jealous of that, to tell you the truth. She could eat whatever she wanted and not gain a pound. Not me. Not with the Ashworth genes." She pointed at the hem. "Too bad about that stain."

Janice decided to brush past that comment. They didn't need to have the conversation derailed by explaining what it was. "Look at this tag," she said, pulling it forward. "It has the initials M.O. on it."

Bronwyn leaned forward and squinted at it. "It sure does." She laughed. "That's crazy. Wait, is this really Marilyn's dress?"

"We're not sure, but we think it might be," Tess said. "I guess that's part of what we're trying to figure out. And when we were talking to your aunt about it, she mentioned that Marilyn had... Well, she basically said Marilyn had kind of disappeared."

"Oh. Yep." Bronwyn laughed. "That's right. I'd forgotten about that."

She sure didn't sound like she was at all worried about what had happened to Marilyn. Which made Margaret's theory more plausible by the moment.

"It's almost funny, isn't it? How secretive everyone used to be about that kind of thing? Now they've got shows on TV all about teen pregnancy, and no one even seems to bat an eye. But yeah, back when we were kids, it was a big scandal. They wouldn't let her marry the baby's father, either, which just made it even worse. He was one of the stable boys, you know. Not exactly the kind of man her parents had in mind. Not that he was interested in marrying anyway. Well, that's why Marilyn was sent away. But you should see that kid now. She's a lawyer and has two kids, and she's doing great."

"So you kept in touch with Marilyn, then?" Janice asked.

"Not at the time, no. Her parents were very good at making sure no one knew how to find her. Though, really, we all knew what had happened, so I'm not sure why they were so secretive. But I didn't reconnect with her until a few years ago, when she found me on Facebook. It's so fun to catch up with her after all this time. And it's so great that it worked out for her just fine in the end. She married a great guy, and she just dotes on those grandchildren of hers."

That could explain how Margaret didn't know they'd reconnected, Janice thought. It had only happened on social media, and only recently.

Bronwyn finally took a breath and cocked her head, looking at them. "So is that what this is about? My aunt thought Marilyn had been kidnapped or something all those years ago?"

"No, your aunt guessed the reason she had been sent away," Tess said.

"Which just goes to show, what's the point, if everyone figures it out anyway?" Bronwyn asked.

"But we found this dress with a few other things in this box," LuAnn explained. "And the other things made us think that somebody might have been in danger."

"Huh." Bronwyn's eyes went directly to the stain on the hem. "Like that bloodstain there?"

"Among other things," LuAnn said. "So we're trying to figure out who the dress might have belonged to."

"Huh," Bronwyn said again. "Well, this might have been Marilyn's dress. But I can assure you that she's alive and well."

She reached into her purse and pulled out her phone. "How about this? Why don't I take a picture of the dress, and I can send it to her and ask if it's hers? I'll let you know what she says. She might have some idea how it could have ended up in that box."

They agreed, and Bronwyn took a few photos of the dress, and especially the tag, and promised to send them to Marilyn. Then they showed her the other items in the box, but Bronwyn didn't recognize any of them. They asked her to look especially closely at the bracelet, which now gleamed in the soft lamplight, but she shook her head. "I'm sorry," she said, "but I don't think I've ever seen that before."

She left a little while later, promising to let them know what Marilyn said. Just as she went out the door, the retired science teachers came in, raving about their dinner at the Boathouse, and then they headed upstairs. With everyone inside for the night, LuAnn locked the front door, and they all headed upstairs. Janice set the box back on the table.

"Well, I guess we can cross Marilyn's name off the list," Tess said.

"Yes and no," LuAnn said, though she dutifully grabbed her notebook from the coffee table and put a check mark by Marilyn's name. "She's not hurt, or worse."

Janice was ashamed at the momentary disappointment she felt. It was a *good* thing that Marilyn was okay, she reminded herself.

"But that dress very well could be hers," LuAnn continued. "And we don't know how it ended up in that box."

"Or how the box ended up in our yard," Tess added.

Janice saw that they were right. They had gotten some answers, but they had only opened up more questions. They would just have to keep digging.

Janice stayed up well past her usual bedtime, looking through the files Brad had brought over from Irene. They were financial records from the properties. Janice tried her best, but no matter how she tried, she couldn't make sense of them. If there was some clue hidden in all this, she wasn't seeing it.

When Janice finally went to bed, she realized that LuAnn wasn't talking to Brad. Most nights, when Janice climbed in bed, she could hear LuAnn chatting on the phone through the wall, but she realized that tonight, Brad hadn't called her.

Janice tried not to think about why.

CHAPTER TWELVE

After breakfast Tuesday morning, two new guests checked in—a minister in town to preach at the funeral of an old friend, and a retired nurse who was visiting family in the area. Janice chatted with them both and found them very pleasant, but her mind was elsewhere, thinking about designer dresses and pocketknives and horse racing. After they'd vanished upstairs, Janice pulled out the phone numbers she'd copied down last night. Of the fifteen names she'd found in the employee files for Dudley's, she'd found only two that were listed in the most recent Marietta phone book—Arthur Dishman and Clarence Reynolds. She supposed she should be grateful to even find those matches, since more than fifty years had passed, and surely most of them would have moved away or, well, passed away. And there was no guarantee these were the same people that had worked in the tavern all those years ago. They could just be people with the same name. But it was worth a shot.

Janice sat down in the small office off the lobby and picked up the phone. She dialed the first number, for Arthur Dishman, and listened as it rang. Voice mail picked up, and a robotic voice told her to leave a message. Janice explained that she was hoping to talk to a former employee of Dudley's Tavern and asked that if she'd gotten the correct person, that he'd call her back. She left her number and hung up.

Then she dialed the number she'd found for Clarence Reynolds. A woman picked up, and when Janice explained why she was calling, the woman said Mr. Reynolds wasn't doing so well these days, but that she would let him know he had a message. Janice hung up, feeling doubtful that she would get a call back from Mr. Reynolds.

She closed her eyes and put her face in her hands. There had to be another way to find someone who had worked at Dudley's. But as much as she wracked her brain, she couldn't think of one.

Janice thought for a moment. There had to be a way to find out more about that box. She got up and wandered over to the filing cabinet and pulled out one of the copies they'd made of Prudence Willard's diary. Janice flipped through the pages. She didn't know what she was looking for exactly. She just knew that the Quaker woman's words, penned so many decades ago, often brought her insight and comfort.

Janice reread several familiar entries about the "packages" Prudence helped shuttle across the border toward freedom. She read a passage about the heartbreak of losing her first baby, a girl, just moments after her birth. And she read about the joy Prudence had felt when her son, Moses, was finally born.

And then Janice's eyes landed on a less-familiar entry. She read it carefully, trying to make sense of it. Prudence was writing about caring for Anna Barton, the woman who had taken her in after she'd escaped from slavery. There was something about a box she'd been looking for, and she seemed to have finally found it. Janice read:

"Today I finally got the box open, and I was not at all prepared for what was inside. I never knew what had happened to the girl—it was almost as if she had simply vanished. And then, to find this..."

What was it, though? Prudence didn't say what she'd found in the box that had led her to understand what had happened to the girl who had disappeared. It wasn't that Janice thought she'd find actual answers in the diary. But this entry had left her even more frustrated.

Janice put the diary pages back into their drawer and decided to do something useful. She grabbed the broom and swept the floor in the lobby. The mindless task gave her time to think, and she was so wrapped up in her own thoughts that she almost didn't hear the phone ring.

"Hello, Wayfarers Inn," she said after racing to the office. She could hear LuAnn and Winnie talking in the kitchen as they worked on making soup for today's lunch, and she knew Tess was cleaning rooms.

"Hello, my name is Marilyn DeForio. Marilyn Oshmann, before that."

"Oh!" It took a second for her mouth to catch up with her mind. "Hello."

"I got an email from my friend Bronwyn Meyers, and she told me you had some questions about an old dress."

"Yes. Yes, we did. Thank you for calling."

"No problem. I have to admit I'm curious. Bronwyn sent me some pictures of the dress you found, and it was definitely mine. I loved that dress and totally remember it. But the initials on the tag really sealed the deal. My mom made me write my initials on all my clothes before camp." She laughed. "So where did you find it?"

Janice wondered what kind of camp involved designer dresses, but decided not to get distracted.

"We found it buried in the yard behind our inn," Janice said. "Along with a number of other objects." Janice named all the other things in the box, but none of them rang a bell for Marilyn.

"I can't tell you for sure how my dress ended up there," Marilyn said. "But I can tell you that we always donated our old clothes to the Salvation Army. There were these bins behind that store, over by the high school? I don't know if they're still there or not. I live on the East Coast now and haven't been back in years. But I would guess that someone bought the dress from the store. I can't even begin to guess how it ended up in the box from there."

Janice thanked her, and she was about to end the call when something occurred to her. Bronwyn supposedly knew Marilyn from the stables, and Bronwyn had said that the father of Marilyn's baby had been someone who worked at the stables.

"I have something of a strange question," Janice said.

"Go for it. I'm loving this trip down memory lane."

"Have you ever heard of a horse named Corona?"

Marilyn laughed. "Wow. That is a strange question. Didn't expect that one. But yes. Of course. He was a big star when I was a teenager. Until, well, you know."

"No, I don't know."

"Until he lost that big race. I forget what it was called. I'd already been sent to live with my aunt by then. I'm guessing Bronwyn told you about that?"

Janice confirmed that she had, and Marilyn went on.

"Well, so I wasn't around when it all happened, but yeah, I was pretty involved with what went on at the stables, so I heard about it, though naturally I can't remember any of the details now. But it was some big race, and everyone expected him to win, but he didn't. There was something about his owners selling him after that, but I don't really know for sure."

Janice asked her if she could think of anyone from the stables whose name started with *L*, or who had a dragonfly bracelet, but she couldn't think of anyone. Janice ended the call, feeling another surge of frustration. So now they knew that the dress had belonged to Marilyn, but that it had been donated to the Salvation Army. Which meant that someone else had likely owned it when it ended up in the box in the yard. Worse, it meant that they'd been distracted all along looking for someone whose initials were M.O., when that likely had nothing to do with whoever was responsible for the box. All Janice really knew was that someone had shopped at a Salvation Army store at some point.

Janice went back to her sweeping and thought about how this new information changed things. So was Peggy O'Neal ruled out at this point? Janice wasn't sure. Just because her initials were no longer a major point of connection, did that mean that her kidnapping wasn't tied up in all this somehow? Janice had tried to fit the pieces together in a way that made sense, and now she tried to rearrange them in her mind, but no matter how she tried, she couldn't make the puzzle complete.

Janice had swept and mopped all the public areas of the first floor when LuAnn came out of the kitchen, a chalkboard marker in hand.

"Wow." She looked around approvingly. "Thank you for handling that."

"I needed to clear my head." She filled LuAnn in on her conversation with Marilyn and what it meant for their search.

"Well, that's a roadblock," LuAnn said with a sigh.

Janice thought it was more than that—it meant that their biggest clue had turned out to have led them astray—but she didn't want to say so.

"I guess we should focus on people whose names start with *L*, not people with the initials M.O.," LuAnn said.

"I suppose so."

Janice put the mop and broom away, but her mind kept circling around the phone call from Marilyn. Something she'd said had stuck in Janice's head, but Janice couldn't figure out what. She stood still for a minute, trying to shake it loose, but nothing came to her. She went upstairs to her room to wash up before lunch, but when she saw her phone sitting on her bedside table she noticed that she had a voice mail. Stacy had called.

"Hi, Mom. It's Stacy." Janice held her breath. "I talked to Dash, and he wanted to know if you want to come by his studio. He'll be around there in the mornings for the next few days, so let me know what day works, and we can set up a time."

Well, that wasn't as bad as she'd expected. If Dash was willing to have her come by his art studio, she would gladly do so.

Janice took a deep breath, said a prayer for grace, and called Stacy back.

"Hi, Mom." Her voice wasn't icy, but it wasn't warm. Janice still had some work to do, that was clear.

"Hi, honey. I'd love to come see Dash's studio." And then, a moment too late, she added, "Thank you."

Janice heard the extension of the inn's phone ring in the next room. Someone must have picked it up downstairs, because it stopped ringing.

"Yep." Stacy wasn't giving anything away. "Okay, how about tomorrow? Dash said that would work best for him."

"Tomorrow it is."

"Great. I'll text you the address."

"I'm looking forward to it."

Maybe Stacy could hear in her voice that this wasn't entirely true, because all she said was, "Okay," before hanging up.

Well, that could have gone better, Janice thought. But at least it was progress.

Please, Lord, mend things between us, Janice prayed. *Help me to show Stacy how much I love her, no matter what.*

Janice sat in her room until the text from Stacy came through with the address, and then she mapped it and saw that it was on the other side of town, in an industrial area that she'd never had much reason to visit. Well, tomorrow she would have a reason.

Janice washed up and started to head back downstairs, but something was still nagging at her. Something about what

Marilyn had said. Janice sat down on her bed and tried to replay the conversation in her mind. It was something about the horse. Something about Corona. Slowly, Janice walked out of her room and over to the metal box, which was sitting on the coffee table. Slowly, she pulled each object out—the dress, which she now knew had belonged to Marilyn. The bracelet, origin still unknown. The matchbook from Dudley's. The letters from L. to a mother she desperately missed. The word *corona*, which Janice now understood was a reference to the horse. There was the knife, which was still with the police. There was the table-cloth itself. And there was the sheet of newsprint.

Carefully, Janice took the sheet of newspaper out of the box and smoothed it on the table. There was the masthead on the front page, and the articles about the nationwide and worldwide news. There was the inside front cover, which had editorials and the weather and the crossword puzzle. There was the inside of the back page, which had the second half of the article about Peggy O'Neal's kidnapping, as well as the article about a hotshot new jockey at Hillsborough Racetrack. Janice read through this one carefully. This had to be it, she thought. This had to be where she'd seen something that was sticking in her mind. The article talked about Marco Kleinman, who was hoping to ride White Lightning, a thoroughbred that had come out of nowhere to win several races so far this season, to victory at the Hillsborough Cup that day. Was this it? Was this the race Marilyn was talking about? The one where Corona had been unseated as the cham-pion? Janice read the article over again, but she shook her head. She didn't know. There just wasn't enough information.

She headed back downstairs to get a bowl of soup—today's special was chicken noodle—for lunch. Mr. Baer, the minister who'd checked in that morning, was marking up some words on a sheet of paper—the eulogy he was writing, Janice guessed—at a table in the corner, and Taylor stood near the kitchen door, ready to help serve. Tess and LuAnn were sitting at a table, bowls of soup in front of them. Janice joined them after getting herself a bowl of soup from the kitchen.

"It's so quiet today, and Taylor can cover one diner, so we figured we had a minute to chat," LuAnn explained.

"What have you been up to?" Tess asked.

"Trying to make sense of a horse race fifty years ago," Janice said, and then explained what Marilyn had told her about Corona and the article in the newspaper page they had.

"It sounds like maybe White Lightning did unseat the reigning champion Corona," LuAnn said. "At least, if Marilyn has her facts right."

"She seemed to know what she was talking about," Janice said. "But how can we figure out for sure if this was the race?"

Tess shrugged. "If this race was that big of a deal, maybe it was in the next day's newspaper."

Had it been? Janice had looked through the June 26 issue of the *Marietta Times* when she looked for information about the Peggy O'Neal kidnapping, but she didn't remember seeing an article about a horse race. Then again, she'd been looking for information about a kidnapping, so she could easily have skipped right over it.

"Let's see if we can get our hands on a copy of the next day's paper," LuAnn said, "and see if we can find any answers there." Then she said, "We just got an interesting phone call."

"What was it?" The soup was delicious and just perfect on this bitterly cold day.

"It was from Sam O'Neal," Tess said. "He called to talk to LuAnn."

It only took a moment for Janice to figure out who that was. "Peggy's brother."

"That's right," LuAnn said. "It was very enlightening."

"Well?" Janice looked at LuAnn expectantly. "What did he say?"

"He started off by saying that for many years he avoided phone calls like ours."

"Not an encouraging start," Janice said.

"Hang on. It gets better." LuAnn picked up her spoon and stirred her soup.

"I suppose that depends on what you consider to be better," Tess said wryly.

"Fair enough." LuAnn scooped up a spoonful of soup and lifted it to her mouth before continuing. "What he said was that he wasn't able to answer questions about his sister's disappearance for decades, but that things had recently changed, and he now felt free to speak openly."

"What changed?" Janice asked.

"Peggy recently passed away," LuAnn said.

"Oh." Janice tried to take this in. "Wait, what?"

"I was confused too. But let me explain. Believe me, it does make sense." LuAnn ate some more soup, and then she continued. "Sam said that when Peggy disappeared, his parents, understandably, freaked out. They all thought something terrible had happened to her, because Peggy and Troy had made sure it looked that way."

"Troy?"

"That was her boyfriend. Though the family didn't know that at the time. He was significantly older, out of college already, and Peggy hadn't introduced him to her family. They didn't know he existed."

Tess, who had already heard this story, nodded. "It sounds like classic daddy issues, if you ask me."

"What do you mean?" Janice wasn't following.

"Well, Sam didn't come out and say this, but he hinted that their father was a bit, well, controlling, I suppose you'd say."

"He was way too harsh with his kids," LuAnn said. "And beat them when they disobeyed. Not just an occasional spank but hit with a belt until blood ran down their legs. That kind of thing."

"In some ways, it's only natural that Peggy would want to get away," Tess said.

"Wait. So she wasn't kidnapped after all?"

"At first they thought she had been," LuAnn said. "She and Troy knocked over her bookshelf and broke a mirror and dragged the sheets off the bed, that sort of thing. They tried to make it look like there had been a struggle."

"But there wasn't," Tess filled in. "Really, she and Troy ran away, and they wanted to throw her family off for long enough to get out of the state. She wanted to go to Hollywood and try her hand at acting."

"Oh dear." Janice could see where this was going now. "So when her family discovered her missing, they called the police."

"They thought she'd been kidnapped," LuAnn said. "It wasn't until several days later, when Peggy and Troy had made it to Los Angeles and she saw the headlines in the newspaper there, that she realized how much trouble she was in. She'd meant to throw her family off for a few days, not become a nationwide news story."

"Did she reach out and tell them she was okay?" Janice asked.

"Yes. But by this point, the family had launched a major investigation and offered a big reward and basically accused a man who'd just been visiting his daughter and new grandson of kidnapping."

"The mysterious stranger," Janice said.

Tess nodded. "The police had figured out who he was and cleared him."

"I guess after all that, Douglas O'Neal didn't want to come forward and say she hadn't been kidnapped after all. That she'd run away because she was afraid of him."

"So he just let people go on believing his daughter had been kidnapped when he knew where she was?"

"He was worried about his reputation and the reputation of his bank. Don't forget, he was a rich man with powerful friends. Apparently they'd seen a huge surge of business in the days after his daughter was kidnapped, and he was worried that it would ruin the business if he told the truth. So instead of coming forward with what they knew, he got one of his friends at the courthouse to seal the court records and file an injunction to stop the press from reporting on the story."

"How could he do that?" Janice asked.

"He couldn't, not legally," Tess said. "I checked this with Carrie after LuAnn got off the phone. It's certainly not legal, but that doesn't mean it couldn't be done."

Janice tried to process this for a moment. "Are you saying that rather than tell the police he was wrong, and his daughter hadn't been kidnapped after all, he made it impossible for the case to be investigated or reported on?"

"That's basically what Sam told me. He said it would be bad for business if people found out the truth." LuAnn took another sip of her soup.

"But the family knew." Janice wanted to make sure she had this right.

"The family knew, but they were forbidden to say anything. And apparently his father's temper was enough to keep Sam from saying anything. And then the next year they moved out of the state."

"Wow." Janice had thought she'd heard some bad stories as a minister's wife, but she was still constantly surprised by how dark human nature could be.

"Apparently it didn't last with Troy, but Peggy loved Los Angeles. She changed her name, and she even got a few bit parts in small films. She never reconciled with her father before he died in the 1980s—"

"How sad," Janice said.

LuAnn dropped her spoon in her empty bowl. "But she did see her mom and Sam sometimes after that until their mom died five years ago. Still, Sam never told a soul what had really happened to his sister. But apparently she recently passed away as well, from lung cancer. And now, finally, Sam feels free to talk about what really happened."

"Wow." Janice tried to wrap her mind around this. "So Peggy O'Neal wasn't kidnapped."

"And Sam was pretty sure the stuff in the box wasn't hers. He didn't think she had any connection to Dudley's or to horses or anything like that."

Janice processed this for a moment. "So she probably doesn't have any connection to this case at all?"

"No, it looks like she probably doesn't," LuAnn agreed.

Janice supposed she was glad to hear that Peggy O'Neal was safe after all. Well, not safe anymore. But the kidnapping that had terrified so many parents in Marietta wasn't really a kidnapping after all. That was a good thing, she supposed. But it did paint a horrible picture of the O'Neal family.

And, more to the point, it meant that they were no closer to figuring out anything conclusive about the box.

As if reading her mind, Tess said, "We've still got Lidia Jankowski. We need to find out more about her."

But Janice hated to think about that. Poor Lidia was the only one they knew for certain had met a dark end. And... Well, Janice hesitated to bring this up, but there was one other lead they could follow.

She looked at LuAnn. "What do you think about talking to Brad?"

"Talking to Brad?" Wrinkles appeared in her forehead.

"Just to see if I read things wrong the other day." Janice knew she had to say this carefully. "Remember how I thought it seemed like Brad reacted when he saw the objects from the box laid out on the coffee table?"

"Yeah, you mentioned that," LuAnn said. "But he doesn't know anything about this stuff. He would have said so if he did."

"You were going to call him to ask," Janice said.

"I haven't had a chance yet," LuAnn said.

Janice waited a moment. "I'm sure you're right." She tried to choose her words carefully. "But could we ask him, just to make sure?"

"It would eliminate the possibility that we've overlooked any potential lead," Tess added. "That's all we're trying to do."

LuAnn's mouth was a tight seam. "I really don't think—"

"You could invite him over for dinner," Tess said.

The mention of dinner made LuAnn pause. Janice wondered if she was remembering how Brad had declined her offer for dinner the night before. And what about how he hadn't called her last night? His behavior had been strange. Surely she could see that this was likely connected?

"I'll ask him to dinner," LuAnn finally said. "And we'll see what happens."

"Excellent," Janice said. And then, just as she started to push herself up to get another bowl of soup, the front door opened, and Randy Lewis stepped into the lobby.

"Hello, Randy," Tess said. "Come in. What can we do for you?"

"I wanted to talk to you all about this," he said, and pulled the pocketknife, wrapped in a plastic evidence sleeve, out of his bag. Tess motioned to the empty chair at a café table, and he sat down. The minister in the corner looked up briefly at the policeman's entrance and then looked back down at his papers. Taylor, standing by the drinks station, barely flinched. He must be used to all the strange things that went on at the inn by now.

"We got the test results back from the lab," Randy said as he set the evidence bag on the table. Janice hadn't seen the knife since they'd given it to the police several days ago. She'd forgotten how delicate it was. "It turns out that the powder along the blade is indeed blood."

Janice tried to hold back a smile, but Tess went ahead and let out a snort. Randy looked from Tess to Janice and back again.

"What?" he finally asked.

"You'll have to excuse them," LuAnn said, shaking her head. "It's just that they had suspected as much. It's nice to have confirmation," she said in a tone that told the others to behave.

"Do you have any evidence that this was used as part of a crime?" he asked. Janice forced herself to bite back the response that this was exactly what they'd asked the police for help with several days ago.

"We're not sure," Tess said. "But if you think this is big deal, wait until we tell you what we found out about Peggy O'Neal."

CHAPTER THIRTEEN

Brad had agreed to meet the ladies at Over the Moon for pizza that evening, and Janice found herself inexplicably nervous as she slid into the red vinyl-covered booth. This was just Brad Grimes—she'd known him for many years, and had gotten to know him much better recently as he and LuAnn had been spending so much time together. But still, she was uncertain how this evening was going to go, and she could sense that LuAnn was on edge, so she concentrated on perusing the menu so she didn't say the wrong thing.

A few minutes past six, Brad slid into the open seat next to LuAnn. He leaned in to give her a peck on the cheek and smiled across the table at Tess and Janice.

"Hello there," he said. "What a nice invitation. This certainly smells better than the leftovers I was planning to have for dinner."

Brad was just a touch too cheerful, Janice noted. He was nervous. Had he guessed why they had asked him here?

"We're so glad you could join us," Tess said. "What do you think about splitting two large pies? A veggie and a meat lovers?"

"That sounds great to me," Brad said.

Tess nodded and folded up the menu in her hands.

A server came and handed out frosty glasses of water and took their order, and then Brad laughed nervously. "I am delighted to be here, but I have to admit I'm a bit curious what this is all about."

There was an awkward silence that lasted a moment longer than it should have. Janice waited for Tess or LuAnn to jump in, but when they didn't, she spoke.

"The other day, when you came over to pick up LuAnn, Tess and I had a bunch of different objects spread out over the coffee table," Janice started.

Brad tapped his straw against the table, pushing open the paper wrapper. "That's right," he said as he pulled the straw out. "You said you'd found the box buried in the yard. What a crazy thing that was. Did you ever figure out where it came from?"

"Not yet," Tess said. "That's kind of what we're hoping you can help us with."

Brad tilted his head, but he didn't say anything. Janice read that as a sign that he knew what was coming next.

"When you came in and saw the objects spread out over the table," Janice said, "I could have sworn that you recognized something. The look on your face changed, and it was like—it was like you knew something."

Brad stuck his straw into the glass of icy water and stirred it around, and then he took a sip. He was buying time, Janice would swear it.

"I told them that of course you didn't know anything, but we've run into several dead ends, so they wanted to check anyway." LuAnn took the lemon from the edge of her glass and squeezed it a bit too aggressively. Lemon juice squirted out over the rim of her glass. "I'm sorry if—"

"No, no need to be sorry," Brad said. He stirred the straw around in the water again, and the ice tinkled gently against the glass. "When I got the invitation for dinner, I thought that might be what this was about." Another deep breath, and more stirring. "And I've been trying to figure out how to answer the question fairly."

They all waited a few moments in silence. A tinny version of Kenny Loggins's "Footloose" was playing over the speakers.

"And then, I finally decided I should just tell you the truth," Brad said. "So yes, actually I did recognize one of the things that was on the coffee table the other night. But at first I wasn't sure. I figured there had to be more than one bracelet with dragonflies on it in the world. So I went back and looked, and I found this."

Brad reached into the messenger bag he'd set on the floor under the table. Janice recognized it as the bag he used for work. Now, he pulled out a manila envelope, smaller than the one he'd brought over from Irene the day before, and opened it. He pulled out a faded color photograph.

"When I saw that my aunt was sending you information about the buildings that used to run along the back side of your property, I figured there had to be a connection. That's where she lived, after all."

He pushed the photograph across the table toward Tess and Janice, and they looked down and saw that it was a picture of a much-younger Brad standing next to a girl with shoulder-length honey-colored hair. Brad was probably twelve or so, if Janice had to guess, and the girl couldn't have been much older. They stood in front of some kind of fence backed by a hedge.

"Aw. Look at you." LuAnn pointed to Brad's too-skinny legs and the lock of dark hair that stood up on the side of his head. He was in that awkward preteen phase when kids are no longer cute but haven't really grown into their bodies yet. He had on khaki pants and a yellow polo shirt, while the girl wore a lavender A-line dress that was far too big for her frame.

"Who is she?" Janice asked quietly.

"El." Brad cleared his throat. "Ella Short. But we all called her El."

El. *L*. It clicked into place as he spoke.

"She was a friend of mine." Brad pointed at the girl's wrist, and they saw it there. A slim silver bracelet with tiny flecks of light blue stone catching the light. "You can't see it very well here, but I dug this picture up to make sure I wasn't remembering things wrong. It's hard to see it well in this picture, but I remember the bracelet. She wore it every day. It had belonged to her mom."

"So you recognized the bracelet," Janice said.

He nodded.

Janice held the photo up and studied it closely. It was hard to tell much of anything in this picture. But Brad seemed sure.

"Why didn't you say something Saturday night?" Tess asked.

"Maybe I should have," Brad said. "But I had to think about it. I wasn't sure if I could."

"Why not?" LuAnn asked.

Brad let out a long breath. "Because I promised not to."

There was a pause, and they waited for him to go on, but he seemed to be struggling to find the words to say.

"Maybe you'd better back up," Tess said. "Who is she exactly, and how do you know her?"

Brad took a sip of his water. "I met Ella when we were in sixth grade. She started hanging around at the park where my friends and I played baseball. It seemed like she didn't have anywhere to be. Eventually, I came to realize that I'd had it wrong, that she hung out at the park because there was somewhere she didn't want to be. But I only learned that later. Anyway, after a while, she asked if she could play, and the other guys didn't want her to, but then she threw a mean fastball, and that was that. After that, she was just one of the guys."

"Except that she wasn't," LuAnn said softly. LuAnn was more perceptive than people sometimes gave her credit for.

"Right. Except that she wasn't," Brad said. "We were... I don't know what you'd call us. More than friends. Certainly less than boyfriend and girlfriend. We were just kids, but we had a connection, I guess you might say."

"She was very pretty," Janice said.

Brad's cheeks pinkened. "I sure thought so. I don't know why she hung out with me. Just lonely, maybe."

"I don't think that was it," LuAnn said.

"Well, anyway, we spent a lot of time talking. She lived with her dad and her aunt, and it wasn't a happy situation. She'd grown up in Columbus and only recently moved to town after her mom left. Just up and took off, leaving her with her father. The aunt moved in to help them along, but things weren't right."

Just then, the server set two steaming pizzas down on metals stands in the middle of the table.

"These look delicious," Janice said, more to ease the awkward silence while the server was there than for any other reason. As soon as she left, they all looked back at Brad.

"What do you mean things weren't right?" Tess asked.

"For one thing, her dad drank a lot. Too much. And he got mean." He helped himself to a meat lover slice, while Janice picked up a veggie.

She winced at the words. She didn't even want to imagine that.

"That's mostly why she hung around the park. She didn't want to go home because she never knew what she was going to find. He gambled too. Sometimes, when he won, he would take them all out for dinner and act like they had all kinds of money to throw around. But when he lost, it was bad. I would bring an extra sandwich for her sometimes, just to make sure she had something to eat."

"What an awful way to grow up," LuAnn said.

"She seemed sad a lot," Brad said. "The only thing she really liked was horses. She had posters of them in her room. She was obsessed with *Black Beauty*. Sometimes her dad went to the racetrack, and she always liked to go with him to see the horses."

"I didn't realize children were allowed at racetracks," LuAnn said.

"I don't suppose they were, technically," Brad said. "But I got the sense her father wasn't really so into rules." He took a bite of his pizza and set the slice down. After wiping his hands on a napkin, he continued.

"But she was so kind, and she made me laugh. She always wore this bracelet, and when I asked her about it one time, she said it was her mother's and it made her feel close to her. I thought it was strange at the time, because her mom had walked out. It wasn't until I got older that I came to understand how you can love someone even when they hurt you."

"And she lived in those buildings at the edge of the property?"

Brad smiled. "Exactly. The same ones you were asking Aunt Irene about."

The puzzle pieces were beginning to come together.

"So what happened to her?" LuAnn asked.

"I don't know," he said. "She always talked about running away. She talked about going back to Columbus to try to find her mom. I don't think she ever totally believed that her mom had really left her. She made me promise I wouldn't tell anyone where she was going if she just vanished one night. It's silly, I know, but when I saw that bracelet Saturday, my first instinct was to keep that promise I'd made to her. That's why I pretended I didn't recognize it."

"That's a worthy impulse," LuAnn said. "Keeping your word."

Brad shook his head. "Maybe it's worthy, but it's also silly. Fifty years later? I don't think I'm obligated to keep that promise at this stage. And anyway, she didn't run away."

"How do you know?" Janice asked.

"Because one day, they were all gone. She and her dad and her aunt just disappeared, overnight."

"Did you try to find her?"

"I did what I could," Brad said. "But I was a kid, and this was pre-internet. We didn't have our own phone line, just a party line that everyone on the block listened in on. There wasn't really anything I could do."

"What about your parents? Did they help?" Tess asked.

"My mom said she'd make a few phone calls. And maybe she did. I don't know." He shrugged. "But truthfully, I think my parents were glad she was gone. She wasn't exactly... They would have preferred I spent more time with the kids in their social circle."

"Ah." Janice saw now.

"Well, anyway, I always wondered what happened to her. I even tried to track her down a few years ago, after Stephanie..." His voice trailed off. His wife Stephanie had passed away a while ago. Janice glanced over to see how LuAnn was handling this, but she seemed relaxed and totally interested in what he was saying. Janice loved that LuAnn was confident enough to not feel threatened by something so long ago. "But I couldn't find any trace of her," Brad said. "I even paid some online service to help me track her down, but they couldn't find her either. It was like she didn't exist."

Janice got a sinking feeling in her stomach at his words. There could have been all kinds of reasons why he hadn't been able to track Ella down. It didn't necessarily mean anything bad. It didn't mean...

She glanced at Tess, whose eyes were wide. She was thinking it too. If her bracelet had ended up in this box, along with the knife and dress covered in blood...

"Brad, do you remember ever seeing Ella wear this dress?" Janice held out her phone and scrolled to the pictures of the dress.

"No," Brad said. "But then, I'm a guy. And I was a preteen guy then." He shrugged. "It doesn't really look like something she would have picked out. She was more of a tomboy, but she often didn't have much of a say. Her aunt would come back with whatever was on sale at the thrift store, even if it didn't really fit or wasn't her taste. Ella complained about it, but what could she do?"

Brad picked up his pizza and took another bite.

"Do you all think the stuff in this box could have something to do with whatever happened to her?" he finally asked.

"I think it's possible," LuAnn said. "It's hard to say for sure. But there are enough connections that it's worth looking into."

Janice hoped, with everything in her, that they were wrong about this. That the box didn't contain clues about what had become of Ella Short. Because based on what they knew, and what Brad had said... Well, Janice didn't think that story had a happy ending.

CHAPTER FOURTEEN

Janice had to double-check the address when she pulled up in front of a two-story brick warehouse building Wednesday morning. A natural gas plant, anchored by three huge metal canisters, was on one side of the building, and a chicken processing plant was on the other. Behind it, Janice had seen as she drove up, there was a series of broken-down wharves that led to a stagnant tributary of the Muskingum River. This was still Marietta, barely, but this was a piece of Marietta Janice had never experienced before.

She looked down at the address on her phone and then at the building in front of her. She couldn't see an address anywhere, but this was where Google had directed her. She climbed out of the car and walked toward the metal door at one side of the building. When she got close, she saw a small sign that said Gindy Artist Studios, and there was an electronic keypad. Stacy had told her to dial #207, and when she did, the door buzzed. She pushed it open and found herself in a concrete stairwell. She held the metal handrail as she climbed to the second floor and walked down the polished concrete hallway until she came to door number 207. It was metal but painted bright orange.

Janice knocked on the door, and a moment later, Dash stood in the doorway.

"Mrs. Eastman," he said, and stepped aside so she could come in. "Thank you for coming."

"Please, call me Janice," she said. His smile didn't seem forced. That was a good sign. "And thank you for having me."

Janice hitched her purse up on her shoulder and looked around. The far wall was mostly windows, which brought in lots of sunshine and made the space feel bright and cheerful. The side walls held canvasses of some sort that were covered in... were those flowers?

Janice moved closer, but no, they still looked like flowers. Pansies, and daisies, and asters, and carnations, but also peonies, and amaryllis, and even delphinium and lilies. They were all blooming right there on the canvas. How had he...?

Janice gasped when she realized what she was looking at.

"You made these flowers out of plastic bottles?" she said, turning toward Dash. They were exquisite. Each petal was delicately formed and painted subtly, carefully, so they seemed almost alive, and held together... Well, honestly, she wasn't sure how they were held together. She couldn't see any glue or wires or anything.

"Yep. And latex gloves, glass bottles I've melted down, all kinds of stuff."

Once he mentioned glass bottles, Janice noticed that the stems of the flowers were made of the finest, most delicate glass. "You melted that glass?" she asked. "How?"

He gestured at a metal box against one wall. "That's the kiln. I just find bottles I want to use and melt them down in there, and then while it's hot, I shape it." He pointed to a rack of tools hung neatly on the wall.

"That's incredible." She looked from the kiln back to the delicate glass stems. They were threadlike, translucent. "Wow. I had no idea." When he'd said he used found objects to make sculpture, Janice had pictured egg cartons stuck to cardboard boxes or something else a child could make. She hadn't pictured this. This was…this was incredible. She examined a rose petal made of what looked like a popped balloon up close. But from a foot or two away, Janice could almost smell the sweet scent. "You're very talented."

"Thank you."

Janice looked at Dash again, really looked at him, and saw that beneath the beard and the… What had Stacy called them? Spacers? Those things in the ears, at any rate. Beyond those, he had warm brown eyes and an easy smile.

"How did you get into making these?" Janice asked.

"I spent a lot of time in the garden in my childhood backyard," Dash said. "My parents were, well, they were always free spirits, I guess. My mom had been a nun, and my dad was an electrician. They met at a protest against the Siege of Sarajevo and fell in love."

"Wow." Janice tried to take this in. "Your mom left the cloister?"

"She did. To marry my dad. I was born a year later and my sister a year after that. They settled on a piece of land in Vermont and tried to live off the land."

"I notice you said 'tried to.'" She smiled.

"Well, neither one of them were experienced farmers. They were more dreamers who hadn't realized how short the growing season is up near the Canadian border." He opened the door of a mini fridge on a counter by the door and pulled out a can of sparkling water. "Would you like one?"

"No thank you." Janice didn't like bubbles in her water. But she gestured for him to go on.

"They divorced when I was eight, and my dad moved back to Ohio, where he grew up. My mom stuck it out in Vermont, and she mostly gave up on farming. But we always had a garden, and in the summer, I loved to be out there."

"How long did you live in Vermont?"

"Through college. And then I moved to New York for a few years. That's where the galleries are, you know, so if you want to be an artist, that's where you go."

Janice supposed that was true, though she didn't really know. Couldn't you be an artist wherever you were?

"That's when I started doing work like this." He gestured at the flower pieces. "Something about all the concrete, and the buildings that block the light, and the gray winter, and the subway, with everyone packed together underground all the time. I missed seeing the sun, and I missed plants. So I decided to start making my own."

"Fascinating." Janice moved to examine a piece on the far wall, which looked like a rhododendron bush growing out of the wall. "And how did you decide to use 'found objects'?" She managed to say the phrase without rolling her eyes now that she'd seen what he did with the objects.

"It's what I could afford." He shrugged. "Rent in New York is expensive. Plus, I was taking classes, so there really wasn't a lot left over for food, let alone art supplies."

"Classes in what?"

"I was interested in the intersection of art and theology. So I was studying at a seminary on the Upper West Side."

That was right. Stacy had mentioned that.

"But you decided not to become ordained?"

He shrugged. "I decided to go for the more lucrative career track, obviously."

She laughed. She had so many questions about his faith, about what it meant to him, about how he practiced it. But she'd promised Tess that she wouldn't grill the man, and LuAnn had warned her that what she thought of as simple questions could sometimes make people feel like she was judging them, hoping to hear the "right" answer. So she decided to save those questions for another time, to get to know him as a person instead of trying to see if he checked all the right boxes.

"Good call." She turned back to him. He was watching her, holding the can of water in one hand. "So when did you move to Ohio?"

"About four years ago, after my dad had a stroke."

"Oh. I'm sorry."

"It's all right. It is what it is. He can't live alone anymore, so I moved here to take care of him."

Maybe Janice shouldn't have been so touched by the answer, but she was. It was just that you didn't often see a young man move home to take care of an ailing parent. It was becoming more and more obvious that she'd misjudged him.

"What will you do with these pieces?" she asked.

"I'm finishing these up for an art fair in New York in a few months. Hopefully they'll sell."

"I'm sure they will." She actually meant it. Janice couldn't quite see how a piece like this would fit into the decor of the inn, but she could see that for the right space, this would be a beautiful piece of art. Like a garden on your wall.

"Dash," she said thoughtfully, remembering Tess's advice. "That's an unusual name."

He smiled. "It's short for Dashiell. My grandfather served on the USS Dashiell during World War II. He died shortly before I was born, and this was how my mom chose to honor him."

"It's lovely."

He shrugged. "I guess I got lucky. His name was Rudolph. I got teased for my name, but not nearly as much I would have if I'd shared a name with a Claymation reindeer."

Janice laughed, and he laughed along too. The skin around his eyes crinkled in an endearing way.

Okay, she decided. Maybe she wasn't all in yet. She needed to get to know Dash better. She needed to see him around Larry more, and find out more about his hopes and dreams for the future, and make sure he truly cared about Stacy and treated her well. But she could admit that she at least saw that she'd been wrong to judge him so quickly and so harshly. She was starting to see what Stacy saw in him.

CHAPTER FIFTEEN

When Janice got back to the inn, Tess was wiping down the tables in the café.

"How did it go?" she asked.

Janice took off her coat and hung it by the door. "It was… You know, it was strangely great."

"I don't see what's strange about it. LuAnn and I were both praying like crazy. I expected as much."

Janice laughed. "Well, thank you for your prayers. I appreciate them. It turns out, Dash is a nice guy."

Tess kept her head down as she ran the rag over the last table. She was too kind to say "I told you so," but Janice could read the look on her face. Instead, she just said, "I'm so glad."

"And I'll have you know I didn't interrogate him. I took your advice and left some things for future conversations."

"I'm glad to hear it. Because based on what you've said so far, I'm sure there are going to be plenty of those."

"You know, I think you're right. I suspect Dash is going to be around for a while, and I'm kind of glad about that."

"Good." Tess finished wiping the table and straightened up. "Now all you have to do is tell Stacy that."

Janice felt her muscles tense. "I suspect I'll need you to pray like crazy for that conversation too."

"We'd be glad to," Tess said. "But you know, it's not really all that difficult to say 'I'm sorry. I was wrong.'"

"It shouldn't be, should it?" But with conversations with Stacy, Janice could never predict how things would go.

"I'll pray," Tess repeated at the same time that the front door opened again. Janice looked up, expecting to see the couple that was supposed to check in today but instead found LuAnn peeling off her coat.

"Oh, Janice. How did it go?" She hung her coat next to Janice's and closed the door.

"It was good," Janice said.

"Of course it was. We were praying," LuAnn said.

Janice smiled but felt a tug of frustration. There were plenty of times she'd prayed for things that hadn't gone well. She'd prayed for Lawrence's safety every time he got behind the wheel of a car, and that hadn't prevented his car from skidding on ice and smashing into a tree. God wasn't a genie who granted wishes if you said the right words. But she bit her tongue. That wasn't going to help things now. And she did believe that God heard their prayers. She just didn't understand the ways He sometimes chose to answer them.

"How did your morning go?" Tess asked, then turned to Janice and explained, "LuAnn was going to find out about Ella Short."

"Well, that was the plan," LuAnn said, crossing the lobby toward them. "But it didn't really work out that way."

"You couldn't find any information about her?"

"None." LuAnn shook her head. "I went to the History and Genealogy Archive—"

"Your favorite place," Tess teased.

"What?" LuAnn shrugged. "I like history, so sue me. Anyway, I couldn't find any record of her. Birth, marriage, death, property—there were no records for any of it. I searched under the name Ella, and Eleanor, and Elizabeth. Even Ellen. None of them turned up anything."

"Brad said she was from Columbus," Janice said. "I wonder if you would have to search the records in... I don't even know what county that is."

"Franklin County," LuAnn said. "Danny said he would call a friend over there and see what he could turn up."

"Well, maybe that will turn up something."

"She has to exist," LuAnn said.

"Did you do an internet search? I'm always surprised at how easy it is to find information about people online," Janice said.

"That's where I started," LuAnn said. "I went through dozens of pages of search results and didn't turn up any record of her."

"Well, we know she exists," Tess said. "There has to be a record of her somewhere. We'll keep looking."

Janice waited a second before she clarified. "We know she exist*ed*."

"Let's stay positive," LuAnn said. "She's out there somewhere."

But Janice wasn't so sure.

"Anyway. While I was there, I also found this."

She reached back into her purse and pulled out a piece of paper. She unfolded it, and Janice could see that it was the printout of a newspaper page. She handed it to Tess, whose eyes widened as she read the date on the masthead. June 26, 1964. Then she pointed to the headline.

"Here." Tess gave the newspaper to Janice, and Janice saw what had gotten them so excited.

WHITE LIGHTNING OUTPACES CORONA TO WIN HILLSBOROUGH CUP, the headline read.

"So this was the race that Corona lost," Janice said.

"Right," LuAnn said. "But we still don't know how that ties in with any of this."

"But it has to," Janice said. "Especially since we now know that gambling on the races was happening at Dudley's, and that Ella's father was a gambler."

"Do you think…," Tess began.

"He must have bet on the race," LuAnn finished.

"And maybe he bet on the wrong horse," Janice said. They were all quiet for a moment, thinking this possibility through.

"But that still doesn't explain how this all ended up in the yard," LuAnn said. The frustration in her voice was evident. Janice felt it as well.

"We'll figure it out," Tess said. "The answer is there. We just have to keep digging." After a pause, she turned to Janice. "In the meantime, Janice, you got an interesting phone call." Her voice was overly cheerful. She was trying to change the subject and the tone of the conversation, Janice knew.

"Oh?"

"From an Art Dishman."

It took Janice a moment to place the name. "Oh! He's one of the guys who used to work at Dudley's."

Tess nodded. "He gave his address and said he'd be around this afternoon after three, if you want to stop by. It's over on the check-in desk."

"Great." It sounded like Janice had an afternoon adventure.

"In the meantime, it smells like Winnie has lunch about ready," LuAnn said.

They all helped get the café set up to serve lunch, and then, when Taylor arrived to help, Janice took a bowl of lentil soup and went upstairs. She had a few hours, and she had an idea.

She spread the files from Irene out first, and as she ate, she flipped through the papers, searching for the one she remembered seeing. There. It was a bookkeeping record of rents paid for the old buildings. At first, Janice's eyes glazed over at the pages and pages of tiny cursive notations—name, amount paid, balance due. There had to be several thousand notations here. But she forced herself to look carefully, and there, in the records for June 1963, she finally found what she was looking for. *Short, Walter.* He had paid a $200 deposit on an apartment, plus $200 for the first month's rent.

Walter. That had to be Ella's father's name. That would give them something else to search for in the archives.

Janice looked at further notations for Walter Short and saw that he was often, well, short on the rent. In December 1963, he'd only paid $175, and in January he'd paid $150. The balance due grew, but Fred Martin hadn't evicted the family. Actually, looking at the balances due accumulated by many of the tenants, he seemed to not have evicted many tenants when he could have. Had he kept them on out of the goodness of his heart? Janice hoped so, though she suspected that it was more likely the hassle of eviction and the fact that some money was better than none that kept those people in their homes. Plus, well, to be honest, even with the money he wasn't collecting, Fred was still pocketing a tidy sum each month. And if what she'd heard was accurate, he wasn't spending all that much on heating the apartments or keeping them maintained.

Janice continued to go through the months, looking at each notation for Walter Short, until she came to July 1964. There was a zero entered for the amount paid, and his balance due had ballooned to more than six hundred dollars. Janice looked for his name in the August records, but there were no more entries for Walter Short.

Janice tried to make sense of this. According to the newspaper they'd found in the box, it had been buried no earlier than June 25, 1964. By July 1, 1964, Walter Short was gone.

Janice had a thought. She stood and walked over to where the metal box was sitting on the counter. She took out the pocketknife, still encased in the plastic evidence bag, and looked at it. She held it so the blade, tucked away inside the case, was pointing toward her. The letter engraved on the handle was clearly an *M*. But then she slowly turned it around. How had they missed this? It was like seeing a gorgeous flower and then seeing that it was really made from garbage and realizing you'd been looking at everything wrong. When the blade was facing away from her—the way you'd hold the knife if you wanted to use it, she realized—the letter engraved on the end was clearly a *W.*

Walter. Suddenly, it was like electricity was flowing through her veins. Janice knew. This was Walter's knife. He had buried it in the yard, along with the bracelet his daughter never took off and a dress that she probably wore.

But what had he done before that?

What had he done to Ella?

May 20, 1861

Prudence set the box in her lap and studied it. It was about the size of a cigar box but solidly constructed of some sort of metal. There was a lock on the front, and it held when Prudence tried to hoist it open. She needed to find the key.

It only took her a moment to realize where to look. The velvet pouch under the loose board. She went to the living room and moved aside the clutch of cash—now significantly smaller after the doctor's visit—and pulled out the pouch. She opened it and tipped the contents onto the table. Anna's wedding ring tumbled out, as well as a few coins and Elias's pocket watch. All of Anna's valuables appeared to be contained here. So what could possibly be in that box?

The last object to tumble out of the pouch was a metal key. Prudence carried it to where she'd set the box and tried it in the hole. It turned, and the box unlocked with a click. She opened the lid and saw that it was filled with papers. She carefully lifted the first few papers and pulled them out. LAST WILL AND TESTAMENT was written across the top of the first one. Beneath that was paperwork about the farm, and the deed to a plot at the Quaker cemetery, next to two others. And then Prudence saw what was at the bottom of the box, and suddenly she understood why finding it had been so important to Anna.

CHAPTER SIXTEEN

Janice drove to Art Dishman's place on the outskirts of town that afternoon. Tess had come along with her, while LuAnn went back to the History and Genealogy Archive to see if she could dig up any records on Walter Short now that they knew his name.

"It's just to the left, up there," Tess said, pointing to a house on a rise at the end of a long driveway. The yard around the house was mowed into neat rows, but the house itself was a dingy white, and the faded brown gutter was hanging off the side of the house at an angle. Paint had chipped off the bottom of the wooden garage door.

Janice pulled into the cracked driveway and parked the car. They both climbed out, and Janice heard a dog barking on the other side of the closed front door. They climbed the cement steps and rang the doorbell. They heard movement inside, and the dog's barking got louder, and then, after a minute or two, the door opened.

"Janice?" Art had a hunched back and leaned on a four-footed cane, but his smile was wide.

"Yes. I'm Janice. And this is my friend Tess."

"It's nice to meet you." He pulled open the door and used his foot to nudge a basset hound aside. "Please. Come in. Beulah, you get out of the way."

Beulah the basset had stopped barking now that she could see they weren't dangerous, and Art slowly shuffled into a living room with a dingy tan couch and a blue recliner.

"Sorry I can't offer you much in the way of refreshments, unless you want some stale crackers. I haven't made it to the store in a little while with this weather."

"We're all right," Janice said. Oh dear. Was this poor old guy going to starve out here?

Art must have seen the worry on her face, because he continued, "My granddaughter is taking me to the store later. She looks out for me."

"I'm glad to hear it," Tess said.

"Anyway, you called about Dudley's, isn't that right?" Art asked.

Janice and Tess both nodded.

"What a place," he said, laughing a bit. "It was a fun job for a twenty-three-year-old. Don't think I'd much care for it now."

"We've heard that it was a… Well, a colorful place," Tess said.

"That's one way to put it."

"Can you tell us when you worked there?"

"Oh sure. I dropped out of college in 1962, and that's when I got the job. And I stayed there until 1965, when I enlisted."

"Thank you for your service," Janice said.

He brushed her comment aside. "I figured a war zone couldn't have been much worse than Dudley's on a Saturday night."

"So you worked there when the Cooks owned the place?" Janice asked.

"That's right. And once they sold it, I stayed on. I liked Lucas. He was a good boss. Fair. And he didn't take any guff from anyone. I guess the place finally closed down when he moved on a few years later."

"You mentioned that it was a bit rough there," Janice said.

"What was it like?" Tess asked.

"Oh, pretty much like you would expect when people who couldn't afford it wasted their money on booze and gambling."

Janice didn't need to spend too much time thinking about that scene.

"Did it ever get violent?" Tess asked.

"Oh sure. The cops were called out pretty much every weekend," Art said.

Janice couldn't imagine why anyone would want to spend time at a place like that, but that wasn't the point right now. "We're particularly interested in someone we believe used to go to Dudley's. His name was Walter Short," she said. "Did you know him?"

"Oh yeah. Walt was one of our most regular customers. Nice guy, but boy, did he have a temper. He lived right upstairs, or maybe in the next building over, I think." Art seemed far away for a moment, and then he nodded as it came back to him. "That's right. His sister lived there too. Ramona... Ramona something. Samuelson, I think. She was a looker, that's for sure. I tried to get her to go out with me, but she never would." He shrugged. "There was a kid too, I think. A girl. Sweet kid. Quiet."

"Ella," Tess said.

"Yeah, maybe that's right. I used to see her walking to and from the building, and I always tried to be nice to her. I felt bad for her, always wearing clothes the wrong size and what-not. With her dad and aunt who clearly didn't give a rat's—" He caught himself, coughed, and said, "Who didn't really take care of her like they should have."

"Do you remember the last time you saw any of them?" Tess asked.

Art thought for a moment. "I think it must have been the night of the fight."

"Of what fight?" Janice asked.

"It was so long ago, it's hard to say for sure, but I think it was about a horse or something like that. Let me think" He put his fingers to his temples. "I think Walt had bet on the wrong horse and lost big, and Hal had won a lot. Bet on some hotshot jockey. Well, Walt didn't take it so well. I don't know what all happened, just that his daughter and sister came down to drag him home, and he was shouting and kicking. I didn't see what happened after that, but they were gone the next day. Up and left in the middle of the night, as far as anyone could tell."

That was it, then. That was the night they'd buried the box and run away from town, skipping out on the rent. But what had happened? Why did the family leave town so suddenly? Had he hurt Ella and tried to bury the evidence? But if so, where was she? Actually, in either case, where was she?

They talked with Art a little while longer but didn't end up much closer to finding answers about what had happened the night the Short family disappeared.

Tess and Janice called LuAnn on the way home from Art's. She was still at the History and Genealogy Archive, and they asked her to also do a search for the name Ramona Samuelson while she was there. LuAnn agreed, and they headed home. Janice helped Tess with the laundry and both worked to clean Moonlight and Snowflakes after the minster checked out. Janice had just started to boil water for rice for dinner when LuAnn came home. She came in the door with her purse slung over one shoulder, carrying a stack of pages she'd printed out.

"It looks like you had good luck," Tess said. She pulled out a chair at the table and gestured for the others to do the same.

"Luck had nothing to do with it," LuAnn said. "I worked hard. And I think I found something."

"What is it?" Janice sat down across from LuAnn.

"Well, first I did some research on Walter Short," she said. "Danny got his friend Mike in Franklin County on the line, since Brad said that Ella was from Columbus originally. Mike helped us dig up a marriage record between Walter Short and Mimi Stierwalt in August 1951. And then Walter was listed as the father on a birth certificate for Ella Leigh Short, born in March of 1952."

"That's her," Janice said. "What else did you find?"

"Things get a little murky from there. There's no other record of Ella Short at all in the records of Franklin County or Washington County."

"How many counties are there in Ohio?" Tess said with a sigh.

"Too many to go through all of them individually, hoping to get a match," LuAnn said. "Plus, we don't even know if she stayed in Ohio."

"But there was no death certificate for her, right?" Janice asked.

"Correct," LuAnn said. "However, if she... If something bad happened to her the night the family left town, it's unlikely they would have reported it."

"I'm going to go with the positive take on this and assume she's still out there somewhere," Janice said.

"Good. I like it." LuAnn shuffled to the next page in her stack. "I was able to find some records for Walter Short, though. He was arrested for public intoxication, driving under the influence, and assault and battery throughout the next decade."

"He sounds like a stand-up guy," Tess said.

"And then I found a death certificate for Walter Short. He died in the Ohio State Penitentiary on September 16, 1974."

"That's awful," Janice said.

"What was he in prison for?" Tess asked.

LuAnn shook her head. "Nothing to do with Ella, as far as we know. A hit and run. He was driving under the influence."

Janice shook her head. She wondered what had happened in Walter's life that had turned him into what he became. What kind of terrible hand had he been dealt that led him to this?

"I also found something for Ramona Samuelson," LuAnn said. She shuffled her papers and pulled out a printout from a newspaper. Janice saw right away that it was an obituary.

Ramona Eunice (Short) Samuelson passed away quietly on May 20, 2017. She will be laid to rest at Franklin Funeral Home at 145 Marcellus Road, Steubenville, Ohio, on Friday, May 23rd.

"That's it?" Tess said. "That's the whole obituary?"

"That's all I could find," LuAnn said.

"What about survivors? What about anything personal?" Tess asked.

Janice didn't need to ask. Lawrence had led several funerals like this, where the person seemed to have no real family or friends. That was what this meant, and it broke her heart. She couldn't imagine letting the people you cared about drift so far away they didn't even come to your funeral.

"At least we know one thing," Janice said instead of answering Tess's question. They both looked at her. "Ramona lived in Steubenville."

"Right," LuAnn said. "Maybe that's where the family went after they left Marietta."

"We don't know that for sure," Tess said. "All we know is that Ramona lived there when she died."

LuAnn nodded. "I wasn't able to find property records or any other tracks for any of them in Steubenville, but that doesn't mean they didn't live there," she said.

"But why wouldn't Ella be listed as a surviving relative?"

"Maybe they didn't get along," LuAnn said. "They might not have been in touch."

Or maybe Ella wasn't around to be listed, Janice thought. She didn't like to think negatively, but she had to follow where the clues led.

"But here's the most interesting thing I found." LuAnn shuffled her papers and found the one she was looking for. "I knew Ella's mother's name—Mimi Stierwalt—and her birthdate—September 25, 1936—"

"From the inside of the bracelet," Janice said, nodding.

"Exactly. So it wasn't hard to find records for her. And guess what I found?"

Janice couldn't even begin to guess.

"Custody petitions," LuAnn said. "Repeated attempts to get Ella away from her father."

"But wait. I thought Brad said that Ella's mother left and didn't want her?" Tess said.

"That's what her father must have told her," LuAnn said. "But the court records say differently. According to the papers Mimi filed, she had some health problems, and while she was in the hospital, Walter filed for divorce and got custody, claiming Mimi was unfit to care for their child."

"Because she was in the hospital?" Tess asked.

That didn't sound right to Janice. "Can I see?"

LuAnn handed the paper to her, and she read it quickly. "Ah," she said. "She was in Overfelt."

"What's that?" Tess asked.

Janice had had occasion to visit church members there once in a while. "It's a mental health facility. Mimi must have had some kind of episode."

"Or been shunted there by a husband who wanted her out of the picture," LuAnn said.

Janice wasn't sure which possibility was worse.

"In any case, she spent two months in Overfelt," Janice said, reading from the paper. "That must have been when Walter told Ella her mom had left."

"How awful," Tess said. "And while she was locked up, that's when Walter filed for custody?"

"And won it, apparently," LuAnn said. "And they moved, along with Walter's sister, to Marietta. And Ella was told all along that her mother had gone off because she didn't want her."

"Meanwhile, Mimi spent the rest of her life fighting to get her daughter back. She died in a car accident in 1972."

"But Ella never knew," Tess said.

Janice thought back to the letters Ella had written to her mom. Hadn't she known? Janice supposed she hadn't, really. But the very existence of the letters showed that Ella—*L*—had still hoped. No matter what, no matter how distant the possibility, a child always wanted to believe her mother cared. Wanted to make her happy.

"We need to find her," Tess said. "She needs to know."

"But how?" Janice shook her head. "We've tried everything we can think of."

Tess looked at each of them. "I think this is our last trail to go down," she said.

LuAnn gathered her papers together. "What do you mean?"

"Think about how much we've learned," Tess answered. "We started out with four possibilities." She held up her hand and started counting on her fingers. "One, Peggy O'Neal. We know she wasn't kidnapped, and that she ran away to California." She held up another finger. "Two, Lorelei, Cynthia's sister. She was too young to be our missing girl." Another finger. "Marilyn Oshmann, who was sent away to have her baby. And four"—her pinky finger went up—"Lidia Jankowski. I don't think we'll ever know what happened to her, but I think we're pretty much agreed that she's not our girl either."

"You're right," said LuAnn. "And now we have one more."

"I hate to say it, but I think the most likely possibility is that we know why Walter buried Ella's things in the backyard of Dudley's before they disappeared that night," Tess said.

Janice absorbed this. Could she be right? Ella Short had simply vanished. Could she have died?

"There has to be some other answer," LuAnn said.

"I'm not willing to give up looking for her either," Janice said.

"I didn't say we should give up," Tess said. "Just that I'm afraid we won't like what we find."

They sat in silence for a minute, thinking. And then Tess said, "I have an idea."

"Really?" Janice tilted her head.

"It's a long shot," Tess admitted. "But I think it's worth a try."

CHAPTER SEVENTEEN

An hour later, Janice sat in the passenger seat while Tess cruised down the highway. It was about a two-hour drive to the town on the eastern edge of the state, and an hour into it Janice still didn't totally understand what their plan was.

"You want to just drive up to a stable in Steubenville and ask if they know Ella?" she asked.

"It's the *only* stable in Steubenville," Tess said, as if that made this whole trip any less crazy.

"But we don't even know if Ella has a horse. And even if she does, we don't know if she would stable it," Janice said. "Maybe she has land and keeps her horse at home. Maybe she doesn't even have a horse. Maybe she doesn't live in Steubenville at all because, oh that's right, we don't even know if she's still alive."

"You didn't have to come with me, you know," Tess said. "You're here voluntarily."

"I couldn't let you try this insane thing on your own," Janice said. "Who knows what kind of trouble you might get into?"

"You'll see. Someone there is going to know who Ella is. Even if she doesn't stable a horse there, even if she doesn't have a horse, someone at the stable will know her."

"What makes you so sure of that?" LuAnn said, shaking her head.

"Brad said she loved horses," Tess said slowly, as if explaining something complicated to a child. "She had posters of them. She went to the track to watch them."

"Yes...." Janice knew where this was going, but she still didn't buy it.

"Little girls who love horses grow up to be women who buy horses."

"I don't know." Janice leaned her head against the car window. "I was a girl who loved David Cassidy. I had posters of him on my wall. But I didn't grow up to buy David Cassidy."

"But given the chance, you totally would have," Tess said with a smile. "All right. I can't promise that she has a horse. But believe me. Horse people are crazy. I had to talk to lots of them at Jeffrey's club"—Tess's husband had managed a golf club in Stow, and Janice supposed there was probably significant overlap between people who had horses and people who joined golf clubs—"and their horses were all these women talked about. What they ate and what was going on with their teeth and what competitions they were going to. I had to pretend I knew what they were talking about and got good at playing along. But all I really learned is that people who love horses *really* love horses."

"Okay," Janice said. "But say she doesn't have a horse."

"Steubenville only has, like, twenty-thousand people," Tess said. "Surely someone will know her."

"Sure. Just twenty-thousand people. How could they not know her?" Janice shook her head. "So we're just going to, what, show people a photo of her when she was twelve and hope someone recognizes her now?"

"Do you have a better plan?"

LuAnn sighed. "The problem is that we don't know that she ever even lived in Steubenville."

"You're right." Tess shrugged. "Worst-case scenario, we enjoy a nice drive to a beautiful small town on a gorgeous day."

Tess was being a tad bit optimistic here, Janice knew. The drive was mostly highway, and it was hardly a sunny spring day. Thick heavy clouds hung low in the sky. Snow was predicted for this evening, but judging by the clouds, it might start sooner than that. But she saw her point. If they didn't find any trace of Ella in Steubenville, they may never find out the truth about how that box had ended up buried in the yard, but at least they would know they had explored every avenue to try to track her down.

They listened to music from their high school days—the Temptations, Carole King, the Bee Gees, the Rolling Stones—until they got to the outskirts of Steubenville, a beautiful old river town with a historic main street. The town had fallen on hard times in recent years, but traces of its former glory were still evident in the detailed brick and masonry buildings and the wide boulevards that crisscrossed the city. The highway skirted the edge of the city, and they took an exit that led away from the city center and toward rolling green hills.

"The stable is three miles that way," Janice said, looking at her phone. They followed the road as it wound its way over hills and through the oak, elm, and maple trees. They passed under an old stone railroad bridge, and then a brown sign with white letters announced HOPEWELL STABLES. They pulled into a small parking area and stepped out. To the left was a wide paddock and to the right several wooden stable blocks. Directly ahead was a wooden building with big windows perched on a rise. The whole area was surrounded by trees that must be gorgeous in the summer.

"Shall we?" Tess grabbed the photo of Brad and Ella—the only picture they had of her—and started toward the door.

"You're not having second thoughts, are you?" Janice asked, climbing out of the car.

"No such luck." Tess started for the building, and Janice followed reluctantly a few steps behind. Tess held her head up high as she pushed open the door, and Janice wished, for just a moment, that she had even just a fraction of Tess's confidence.

Tess made her way directly to the wooden desk. The walls were surfaced in rustic stone and held up with rough-hewn beams.

"Hello." The woman behind the desk had curly brown hair and a wide smile. "How can I help you?"

"We're hoping to talk to one of your members," Tess said. "And we hoped you could help us."

"Who are you looking for?" the woman asked. Janice guessed her to be in her midforties, with an accent that said she originally came from farther north. Michigan, or maybe Minnesota.

"Ella Short," Tess said confidently.

"Ella Short?" The woman's brow creased. "I'm sorry, I don't know an Ella Short."

Janice felt vindicated. This whole thing had been one big crazy wild goose chase.

But Tess was undaunted. "I'm sorry, she may go by something different now," she said. "Maybe Eleanor? Or Elizabeth?"

Again, the woman shook her head. Tess turned to Janice. "I'm having a senior moment, Janice. Do you remember her married name?"

Janice panicked. Why was Tess asking her? She shook her head. She was going to kill her when they got back to the car.

By now the woman at the desk was getting suspicious. "Can you tell me why you were hoping to get in touch with this member?" she asked.

"An old friend is trying to get in touch with her," Tess said smoothly. "We're trying to help him find her. See?" She pulled the photo of Brad and Ella out of the envelope and shoved it across the desk. "That's our friend Brad. They were childhood sweethearts, and he's never really gotten over her."

Janice wasn't sure this was true—Brad had married, and he was dating LuAnn now, after all—but she decided not to say anything. Tess was on a roll.

"We're hoping to track her down, and we thought we had tracked her here. Do you recognize her?"

The woman pulled the photo closer.

"Huh," she said.

"Huh?"

"That almost looks like Leigh Circone."

Tess's eyes narrowed, and she glanced at Janice. But Janice didn't need her look to pick up on it. She'd heard it too. Leigh was Ella's middle name.

"Hey, Kelly, can you come out here a second?" the woman behind the desk called.

A moment later, a woman with dark hair pulled back in a ponytail came out of a door Janice hadn't noticed to the right.

"These women are looking for someone for an old friend. It's her." She pushed the photo across the desk toward Kelly. "Doesn't that look like Leigh?"

"Wow." She studied the photo, and a smile spread across her face. "It does look like her." She looked up at Tess and Janice. "What is it you were looking for?"

"We were hoping to get in touch with her," Tess said.

"I'm sorry," Kelly—she seemed to be the manager—said. "I'm afraid we can't give out information about our members."

"I'd expected as much," Tess said. "Would it be possible to leave her a message? Here." She reached into her purse and pulled out a business card for Wayfarers Inn. "May I?" She pointed at a ballpoint pen on the desk.

"Of course," the first woman said.

Tess used the pen to write *regarding Bradley Grimes* on the back, and left it with the woman.

"Thank you so much," Tess said, setting the pen down on the desk again. "We really appreciate your help."

Tess waited until they were back in the car before she pumped her fist and laughed out loud.

"Okay. I'll admit it," Janice said. She still couldn't quite believe it. "Your crazy plan worked. Now we just have to see if she calls us."

"No we don't," Tess said. Janice looked and saw that she was already using her phone to google the name Leigh Circone. "What do you say we go talk to her right now?"

May 22, 1861

Anna sat propped up against the pillows. A little color had come back into her cheeks, and her hair was brushed away from her face. She was wearing a clean nightgown, and she looked more peaceful than Prudence had seen her in days.

"I am glad thee was able to find it," Anna said after Prudence had explained the search for the metal box.

"Thee first told me it was in the hayloft," Prudence said with a laugh.

"Elias did keep it there for a while, but after he passed, I brought it inside the house," Anna said, shaking her head. "I must have been trying to explain that. Though I can't tell why I thought that would be important."

"The fever was speaking," Prudence said.

"I moved it in here when I started to feel poorly, so it would be close by. But I guess I forgot to tell thee that part."

Prudence laughed softly.

"It is normally kept in the closet under the stairs," Anna said. "In case thee needs to find it in the future."

Anna was referring to the will and testament, Prudence knew. "I will not need it anytime soon."

"No, it looks like I may yet live a while," Anna said with a smile. "But it was when I wasn't sure that I realized what a horrible mistake I'd made."

"Thee did what thee had to do," Prudence said.

"No, I did the cowardly thing." Anna looked down at the small frame in her hands. "It seemed easier not to talk about her, because doing so brings it all back. But what I realized as I lay here was that after I am gone, there will be no one left who knows her story. No one to remember her. All because I was afraid to feel sad."

Prudence gazed at the daguerreotype in the oval frame. It showed a girl with golden curls and a light in her eyes that came through even in the black-and-white print. Most daguerreotypes showed serious, somber people, but Faith looked like she was about to burst into laughter. Prudence knew that losing her young daughter to illness had been the lowest point of Anna's life. She had never recovered from it—something that Prudence could herself understand, having lost her own sweet Hope only moments after her birth. But Anna had never spoken about Faith, never shared much of anything about her life with Prudence. Prudence had always understood that the grief was too raw and that talking about her lost daughter only made the pain fresh all over again. But Prudence knew so little about the girl. It was almost as if she had simply vanished, leaving a hole in Anna's life that Prudence had done her best to fill. Now, however, something seemed to have changed.

"I do not want Faith to be forgotten," Anna said. "I want to tell thee about her so that she will live on in memory after I'm gone."

"And I would love to hear about her."

Anna spent the next thirty minutes or so telling Prudence stories from Faith's life, about her first words and the way she'd tumbled from the tree when she was three and not even shed a tear while Anna reset her shoulder. About how she'd loved to chase the birds, and drink fresh milk straight from the bucket and how she could remember songs the first time she heard them. The little girl who had been but a shadow, a ghost, to Prudence, now took on flesh and bones. Anna talked as long as she could, but she soon tired. The effects of the fever had not passed yet.

"It is all right," Prudence said. "Thee will tell me more about Faith tomorrow."

"Yes," Anna said. "I will."

"And I will not forget her," Prudence promised. "I will tell my children about her."

Anna smiled, leaned back against the pillows, and closed her eyes.

"She will not be forgotten," Prudence promised, before she stood and quietly made her way out of the room.

CHAPTER EIGHTEEN

Janice glanced at the door. She had arrived at Jeremiah's early, and she had five minutes before their agreed time, but she still wasn't convinced Stacy would come. She went to the counter, ordered a vanilla latte, and sat down at one of the wooden tables by the window. At three minutes past two, Stacy appeared in the window. She had her scarf pulled up over her nose and her hat pulled down, but it was her.

A gust of cold wind blew in, and Stacy shut the door and stomped her boots before coming over to Janice.

"Let me get you something," Janice said.

Stacy scanned the board above the counter. "How about a matcha latte?"

"Sure thing," Janice said, though she had no idea what a matcha latte was. But the guy behind the counter seemed to understand the order, and a minute later, Janice was holding out a foamy green drink to Stacy. Who wanted green coffee?

"What is that?" Janice asked when Stacy took it.

"Green tea."

"A green tea latte?" It sounded terrible. But that was okay. She didn't have to like it. If Stacy liked it, that was all that mattered.

"It's good. You want to try it?" She held the cup out so Janice could take a sip.

Janice wanted to want to try it. She wanted to be the kind of person who got excited about putting green tea in coffee. But she just wasn't.

"That's all right," she said. "I'll stick to my latte. But I'm glad you like it," she added. "That's what's important."

Stacy gave a knowing laugh.

"Where's Larry?" Janice asked.

"A playdate," Stacy said.

Janice nodded, and then she tried to figure out the words to say what she'd come here to say.

"I like Dash," she finally said. "I thought his art was beautiful, and he seems like a great guy. I judged him wrong, and I'm sorry about that."

Stacy's shoulders unhitched a bit. "He really is great." She wrapped both hands around the paper cup.

"I like him, and I want to get to know him better."

"I'm glad."

"But that's not really what I wanted to say to you," Janice continued. "What I wanted to say is, I shouldn't have judged him at all. I didn't realize that I had been carrying around an idea in my head of the kind of man I thought you should marry, but I did. And that idea was not based at all on who you are but on what I thought I wanted."

Stacy was nodding, listening intently.

"But what I really want, more than anything else, is for you to be happy. For you to find a man God approves of and to let that take priority over whatever preconceived ideas I may have. I guess what I'm trying to say is, you are a smart, capable, beautiful, strong woman. And I'm finally realizing that I need to trust you to make your own decisions and to support them instead of inserting myself into them all the time."

Stacy looked down at her cup. Janice could have sworn she saw tears gathering in her daughter's eyes, but she blinked them away.

"Thank you," Stacy finally said. "I appreciate it."

Janice waited for her to go on, but she didn't. Maybe she didn't have any more to say. Maybe she didn't know what to say. In any case, Janice knew it wasn't a magic pill. The hurt and disappointment in their relationship ran deep enough that it wouldn't be easily fixed by one apology. It would take years of working at it, Janice knew.

But she also knew that no matter how deep their misunderstandings ran, their love was deeper. When Janice looked at her daughter, she felt a love more powerful than anything else on this earth. Nothing in the world would ever keep her from loving her daughter, and nothing would keep her from trying to make their relationship better. Even if it meant admitting when she'd been wrong.

Stacy finally looked up and gave her a smile, tears in her eyes.

It would take a lifetime of work, but every moment was worth it.

CHAPTER NINETEEN

A fire was roaring in the hearth, and the lobby of the inn was cast in a warm, cozy glow on this dreary Saturday afternoon. Tess kept peeking out the front window, hoping to catch a glimpse of their car, and Janice kept sneaking bites of the lemon cookies LuAnn had baked. The only one who seemed relaxed as they waited was Brad, and he was the one who had the most to be excited about.

"The weather probably slowed them down," Tess said.

Janice nodded, even though the roads had been cleared of Wednesday's snowstorm for days. She'd finally finished the jigsaw puzzle as the snow swirled around them, making the summer scene depicted on the puzzle pieces seem further away than ever. But it had been satisfying to finally see the picture come together. And hopefully, soon, another one would.

"It's still five minutes to three," Brad said. "They'll be here." Brad was sitting in one of the wingback chairs in the lobby, flipping through a magazine that showcased local people and places. He appeared to be reading an article about a corn maze from last fall.

At last, a gray station wagon pulled into the driveway, and Leigh—Ella—and her husband, Rob, stepped out. Janice and Tess had met Leigh when they'd been in Steubenville earlier in the week. To say Leigh had been surprised to meet them had been an understatement, but once they showed her the picture of her and Brad and showed her photos of what was now Wayfarers Inn, she was curious. She'd explained that she'd started going by her middle name after the family had moved to Steubenville—she'd tried to create distance from her life before.

And she was here in Marietta today to finally, after all this time, answer some questions about what had really happened the night she and her family had buried a box in the yard and fled Marietta. Janice knew they all hoped she would find some closure—and they hoped they would too.

Janice watched through the front window as Leigh took in the inn and the wide, empty yard behind it. The construction equipment was gone, and though the yard was still torn up, there was nothing between the inn and the alleyway, where the buildings once stood. She couldn't imagine what it must have looked like the last time Leigh had seen it or what kinds of memories it brought up to be here again. Leigh stood still for a moment, and then she turned and took her husband's arm, and together they walked toward the door.

Leigh still had the same golden hair she'd had in the photo, but now it had streaks of gray and was cut into a stylish bob. She wore a long camel-colored coat and a red scarf. Her husband was tall, with a square jaw and dark hair threaded with gray. They cut a striking picture as they walked up the steps and rang the doorbell.

Tess pulled the door open and smiled as she welcomed them inside.

"This is just beautiful," Leigh said, looking around the room. "To think you've done all this with that old warehouse." She shook her head, and then she spotted Brad.

Brad walked toward her and wrapped her in a hug.

"Oh my goodness. Bradley Grimes." Leigh wrapped her arms around him again. "I never thought I'd see you again." They held each other for another moment, and then she pulled back, taking him in.

"Oh my goodness. You look just the same." She laughed, a sweet, warm laugh.

"I sure hope not," Brad said.

"Here." Leigh reached out and took her husband's hand. "Brad, this is my husband, Rob. Rob, this is Brad, one of my oldest friends."

Rob stuck out his hand, and he and Brad shook, with what seemed to be genuine smiles on both of their faces. Tess then introduced LuAnn to both of them, and they all shook Rob's hand. Then they all sat down around the coffee table.

"Oh my," Leigh said as she saw the metal box that had started all of this. "That's it, huh?"

"This was found in the yard," Tess said, pointing to the box. "Over behind where those old buildings used to stand."

"I recognize it," Leigh said. "It was once where my aunt Ramona kept important papers and things." She shook her head and carefully lifted the lid. "Wow."

She was still, staring down at the contents of the box for a few moments. Rob put his hand on her back.

"I never thought I'd see this again," she said, reaching into the box. She pulled out the bracelet and clutched it in her hands. There were tears in her eyes. "This belonged to my mother."

"We know," Tess said gently.

"Thank you," Leigh said, "for finding it." She set the bracelet down and pulled out the dress and held it up. "Wow." She shook her head. "I remember this. I'd forgotten I was wearing it that night."

"We tracked down the original owner of the dress, and she said you'd probably gotten it secondhand," LuAnn said.

Leigh nodded. "Pretty much all my clothes were from thrift stores. I think my aunt must have gotten this on sale. It was far too big for me." She eyed the stain at the hem, pressing her lips together.

She picked up the rest of the objects in the box, one at a time, and they all gave her space to examine each one. She pulled the letters out of the envelopes and read them, fighting back tears. "My mom was the first one who called me El," she said softly. "I don't know when we shortened it into the letter *L*, but that's how she wrote my name." Leigh paused for a good long while, looking down at the knife encased in a plastic bag. The fire crackled in the hearth, and the clock on the mantel ticked softly. Then, finally, she set the knife back on the coffee table and spoke.

"I guess you're probably wondering what all of this was doing in your yard?" She had a resigned smile on her face.

They all laughed nervously. Truthfully, they'd already pieced most of it together, but they wanted to hear it from her to make sure they had it right.

"It's not a happy story," she said. "Most of my memories from this time in my life weren't happy." She smiled shyly at Brad. "Brad was the one exception. Otherwise, this was a pretty rough time."

"I'm sorry if this brings it all back," Janice said.

"Oh, it's all right. I'm glad for the chance to face it all again, to try to make sense of it."

She took a deep breath, and then she continued. "I grew up outside Columbus. My dad worked at a factory there. He met my mom at a tavern. I don't know that they would have gotten married if my mom hadn't gotten pregnant, but that's how these things sometimes happen, I guess. They were young, and we were poor, and my parents fought, but we were happy enough. Then my aunt Ramona moved in, and things started to change. She'd gotten a divorce, and she was just going to stay long enough to get back on her feet, they said. But she and my mom didn't get along. My dad sometimes took her side. They fought more.

"Then, Mom had a miscarriage and ended up having a… Well, they said she was sick, but I suppose the truth is that she had a nervous breakdown. She went to the mental hospital for a while, and then she decided she didn't want to be a parent anymore. She gave up her custody rights for me."

Janice and the others knew this wasn't true, but instead of interrupting her to correct her now, they let her go on. They would tell her soon enough that she'd believed a lie her whole life.

"So my dad brought me and Aunt Ramona here. He got a job working in shipping that I guess paid more. We lived in this awful apartment over a noisy bar. He drank too much and gambled away most of what he earned."

"At the racetrack," LuAnn said gently.

"And at the bar. You could place bets there too. But I preferred the track, because sometimes he'd let me go with him. I loved to watch the horses. I got to know the people who worked at the stables. Sometimes they'd let me pet the horses and brush their manes. That's where I started to fall in love with horses."

She picked up a cookie and placed it on one of the cloth napkins LuAnn had set by the plate. She took a bite, chewed, and then continued.

"We didn't know it then, but it was around this time that he lost his job. Showed up late or drunk one too many times, I guess. But there was a big race coming up, one he was sure his horse was going to win. He gambled everything he had left on the race."

"Corona," Tess said.

"Yep." She nodded. "I guess you know how that one worked out, then."

"Corona lost," LuAnn said.

"And my dad lost everything. Which was bad, obviously. But the real trouble started that night at the bar. I guess there were some guys who had bet on a different horse, the one that won, and they were being kind of obnoxious about it. That's what he said anyway. I don't really know. All I know is that when Ramona and I came down to get him, he was fighting with some guy."

She reached out and picked up the knife.

"He stabbed someone, didn't he?" LuAnn said.

Leigh nodded. "I don't even know why he'd brought his knife with him that night. But he had, and before we knew what was going on, he'd cut the guy pretty badly in the stomach. He was bleeding a lot. Dad saw what he'd done, how bad it looked, and he just ran off."

"And left you and your aunt standing there?"

"Oh, we didn't stick around. We thought my dad had killed him, and Dad thought so too. We ran back up to the apartment. Aunt Ramona took the knife and made me give her the dress I was wearing because someone might recognize it. She tossed everything on the table and just grabbed the whole tablecloth and tied it up and shoved it all into the box."

"So the other things in the box…," Janice said.

"Just happened to be on the table when she needed some way to dispose of everything," Leigh said. "Including the bracelet I'd taken off that afternoon after the clasp broke and the letters I thought I was secretly writing to my mother. But Ramona didn't stop to look. She just tossed everything in the box and buried it in the backyard. Hiding the evidence, she said. Then she grabbed everything valuable she could find, which wasn't much, and we left."

"Where did you go?"

"It turns out they had a backup plan, in case things got bad. They planned to meet up at my grandparents' old cabin in the woods way outside Steubenville. It was a summer cabin, and it wasn't heated or insulated. There was no running water. But they knew it would be empty. So we lived there for a while."

"For how long?" Brad asked.

She shrugged. "A year, maybe. My dad spent most of the rest of that time in and out of jail. The guy in Marietta didn't die, thank goodness, but Dad got arrested for a DUI and a hit-and-run, and the assault charges caught up with him."

"So you lived with your aunt?" Tess asked.

"For a while," Leigh said. "But as it turned out, she didn't have my best interests at heart. So I left. I was sixteen by this time, and I decided I would be better off on my own. I started using my middle name, lied about my age, got a job, and decided to make my own way in the world."

"But what about child protective services?" Janice asked. "Didn't someone take you in?"

Leigh gave her a sad smile. "Have you ever spent much time out in the really rural parts of the state?"

Janice shook her head.

"I grew up mostly in the hollers of West Virginia," LuAnn volunteered. "I get it."

"It's not that they don't want to help," Leigh said. "It's just that there's too much need and not enough resources."

"Exactly," LuAnn said.

"Anyway, I made it all right. I found a job as a receptionist for a doctor's office. I went to school at night, got my GED. Eventually I made it to college and met Rob, and here we are."

She reached out and squeezed her husband's hand. Janice wasn't sure how much of this story he'd heard before, because he seemed to have that same shell-shocked look that Brad had.

"So that's the story," Leigh said. "Like I said, it's not a nice one. But I am thankful to you for finding these things and for tracking me down." She reached out and picked up the bracelet. "This, especially." She turned it over in her hands. "I know my mom stopped loving me, but I never stopped loving her."

"She didn't," Janice said. Leigh looked so startled that Janice realized it must have come out very strangely. "What I meant to say is, she didn't stop loving you. And she didn't stop fighting for you."

"Okay, fine, people have told me she was sick, she wasn't right in the head, that she loved me as best she could, all that stuff. But she gave up her parental rights, so there you go."

"She never gave up her parental rights," Tess said.

"But—" Leigh shook her head. "Yes she did."

"You father told you that, right?" Tess asked.

Leigh nodded.

"Your father lied to you," LuAnn said gently. "While your mom was sick, he got her rights taken away. But she fought to get them back. We found the court records. Your mother petitioned the court to get custody back over and over again. Until the day she died, she never stopped trying to get you back."

"Is that...?" Her voice came out in a whisper. She tried again, a bit louder this time. "Is that true?"

Rob reached over and took her hand, lacing his fingers between hers.

"It is." Janice pulled a tissue from the box on the table and handed it to her.

"Wow." Leigh looked down at her lap. The rest of them stayed quiet, giving her time to process this. Janice knew it meant seeing everything she'd thought she'd known about her life in a whole new way. Not only did it mean she had to change what she'd always believed about her mother, she now knew that her father had lied to her, repeatedly, throughout her life. "Why didn't I know about this?"

"She didn't know where you were, at first," LuAnn said. "But then it appears that once she did track you down at the address outside Steubenville, your father filed a restraining order, so she couldn't contact you."

"But she kept fighting in the courts, right up until she passed away in 1972," Janice said.

The look on Leigh's face told them all that she hadn't known.

"I'm sorry," Janice said softly.

Leigh bit her lip, fighting back tears. "I mean, I knew she must be gone by this point, right?" She dabbed at the corner of her eyes with the tissue. "But I never knew for sure. I thought it was better not to know, in some ways, because of all the dark thoughts it opened up. But now..." She wiped the tissue across her eyes again. "Now, I just wish I'd tried a little harder."

"It's not your fault," LuAnn said, her voice firm. "None of this is your fault."

They were all quiet for a few minutes. Leigh sat still, clutching her mother's bracelet, no doubt contemplating her new reality. LuAnn had her eyes closed, and Tess was looking down at her lap. Praying, Janice knew, both of them praying. Janice also closed her eyes, and asked for God's mercy and grace on Leigh as she reimagined what she thought she'd known about her family and her life. She prayed for strength for her as she made sense of what she'd just been told. And she thanked God that the truth, after all this time, had finally come to light.

It would be a long road ahead for Leigh, she knew. So much history had been uncovered, and it changed everything.

But then, the truth usually did, Janice knew. When so much had been based on assumptions and lies, the truth could be hard to see. It was difficult to realize that you'd been thinking of everything wrong.

But it was also freeing. She thought about Stacy and Dash. She may have gotten it wrong at first, but she would try to see Dash for who he was, and not who she wanted him to be, going forward.

The Bible says, *"The truth shall set you free."*

Janice had never believed that more than she did right now.

Dear Reader,

I have a friend who loves nothing more than to work jigsaw puzzles. She will sit in her Brooklyn apartment with its picture windows looking out over Manhattan and do puzzles all day. I love that she does this. I don't understand it, but I love it.

I have to admit, I don't have the patience to do jigsaw puzzles. (You already know what it's going to look like. What's the fun in that?!). I don't much enjoy crossword puzzles or Sudoku either. I want to say that I'm just not a puzzle person.

Except that that's not entirely true, because a puzzle was where this story started. *What if...* I started wondering, *they found something, and had to figure out whose it was and how it got there....* And slowly, the individual pieces came together. A missing girl. Evidence that something bad had happened to her. A few red herrings, to make the puzzle harder to solve.

In the end, I quite enjoyed putting the pieces of this puzzle together. I hope it's as much fun for you to read as it was for me to write.

Best wishes,
Beth Adams

ABOUT THE AUTHOR

Beth Adams lives in Brooklyn, New York, with her husband and two young daughters. When she's not writing, she spends her time cleaning up after two devious cats and trying to find time to read mysteries.

DUDLEY WOODBRIDGE JR.

Wayfarers Inn is loosely based on a real building in Marietta, Ohio, one that really was used as a stop on the Underground Railroad. Though we've made changes to the building for this series—it is not an inn in real life, for example—it was fun to explore the real history of the man who ran the first business out of the structure in this story.

The building itself was constructed in 1826 by Colonel Joseph Barker, who designed and built many of the buildings in Marietta. But it was built for Dudley Woodbridge Jr., whose father, Dudley Woodbridge, was one of the first dry goods merchants in the Northwest Territory. The elder Woodbridge came to Ohio from Connecticut in 1789 and started the business, while Dudley Jr. and his brother William (later the first Governor of Michigan) were left in prep school in the East. The younger Dudley eventually moved to Ohio and grew his father's business, and eventually outgrew the building on the banks of the Ohio River. After he moved his headquarters, the building was later used as a hotel, saloon, a liquor store, a factory, and a warehouse over the years.

The buildings at the rear of the property, where I've located Dudley's tavern, are entirely fictional, but I named the establishment Dudley's as a nod to the man who made this part of Ohio what it is today.

LuAnn's Butternut Squash Soup

This soup is really easy and tastes delicious. It's perfect for a cold winter day with a slice of thick bread slathered in butter.

2 tablespoons butter
1 medium onion, chopped
1 large (2–3 pound)
    butternut squash, peeled,
    seeded, and chopped
    into 1-inch cubes

6 cups vegetable stock
½ teaspoon freshly grated
    nutmeg
salt and fresh ground pepper
    to taste

Melt the butter in a large soup pot over medium heat. Add the onion and cook until softened and translucent, which will take five to seven minutes. Add the squash cubes and the stock and bring to a boil. Let simmer for 20–30 minutes or until the squash is soft. Use an immersion blender to puree, and season with nutmeg, salt, and pepper. Serve piping hot.

Read on for a sneak peek of another exciting book
in the Secrets of Wayfarers Inn series!

CROSSING THE RIVER
by Leslie Gould

The lights flickered in Wayfarers Inn as the howling wind shook the windowpanes all through the first floor. Another gust caused the lights to flicker again, but thankfully they didn't go out. It was just after noon, but the day was so dark it appeared to be near dusk. March had definitely roared in like a lion.

LuAnn grabbed the flashlight from under the counter and a pair of cotton gloves and headed down to the basement. Maybelline Rector, the director of the Marietta Underground Railroad Museum, had called a couple of days ago, asking if there was any Harriet Beecher Stowe memorabilia at the inn. She was planning an exhibit to celebrate the 170th anniversary of the writing of *Uncle Tom's Cabin*.

LuAnn was pretty sure they'd already turned over everything they'd found—a clipping of a review in the *New York Times* when the book was first released in 1852, a flyer about Harriet Beecher Stowe speaking in Cincinnati in 1858, and an 1859 article from *Freedom Rings*, an Abolitionist magazine, describing how the death of her sixth child, a son named Samuel Charles, from cholera in 1849, gave her empathy for slave women who lost their children and partly inspired the story. If there was anything more, LuAnn would remember. Harriet Beecher Stowe was one of her favorite historical figures.

But LuAnn told Maybelline she'd look again, and she expected a follow-up call any moment. Maybelline said a staff member from the Harriet Beecher Stowe Museum in Cincinnati was in town to help her plan the exhibit, and she wanted to have everything possible on hand for him to look at.

As LuAnn reached the bottom of the stairs, the lights flickered again. She continued on to the wooden box that had newspaper clippings and old programs and church bulletins in it. She put the flashlight down and slipped on the gloves—not that there was anything in the box worth saving. They'd already rescued anything of value. The remaining papers were old and crumbling, but she didn't have the heart to throw them away.

She began sifting through the documents, reading snippets of wedding-day articles and obituaries and church potluck announcements. Sure enough, there wasn't a thing about Harriet Beecher Stowe. She stood, stretching her back, and peeled off the gloves. Just as she did, the lights flickered again, but this time they went completely off.

She reached for the flashlight but fumbled it, and it fell out of her hand, casting a beam of light into a section of the rock wall that had partially crumbled and was on the list of things that still needed to be repaired. She couldn't be sure, because the flashlight went dark when it clattered to the floor, but

LuAnn thought she'd caught a glimpse of something between the stones, like a package.

She bent down to pick up the flashlight and flipped the switch a couple of times, but nothing happened. Then she hit it against her palm. Still nothing.

She took her phone from her sweater pocket and pressed the flashlight app, stepping closer to the wall. There *was* something pushed back between the two walls of stones and wrapped in a dark material. She reached, straining to touch it. Finally she grabbed a corner of the package and yanked, moving it forward a few inches. She pulled again and managed to get it all the way out.

The material around the package turned out to be a raincoat, wrapped tightly with rusted wire that broke apart as she unwound it. The rubbery material of the coat flaked as she pulled it off. Under the raincoat were several layers of butcher paper that were in surprisingly good shape. As she pulled the paper off, the lights flickered back on to reveal a picture in an oak frame with ornamentation around it, about three feet by two feet or so. She recognized the scene right away—it was of the character Eliza, from *Uncle Tom's Cabin*, fleeing across the frozen Ohio with her child, Little Harry, in her arms.

Carefully, LuAnn ascended the stairs to the lobby, with her gloved hands tightly gripping the picture frame. She bumped the unlatched door open with her hip and called out, "Look what I found!"

Tess's copper-colored hair was pulled back, giving LuAnn a clear view of the surprise on her face. "What in the world did we miss down there?" she asked as she stepped around the counter.

"You're never going to believe this." LuAnn turned the picture around.

The surprise on Tess's face turned to confusion. "What is it?"

"A scene from *Uncle Tom's Cabin*. Don't you recognize it? Eliza on the frozen Ohio River."

"Not at all." Tess gave her a sassy grin. "I never read *Uncle Tom's Cabin*."

"What?" LuAnn couldn't contain her shock. "That's un-American. I thought everyone had read it."

"Everyone who's a history major," Tess shot back. "Or taught English." She leaned against the counter. "Let's take a poll. I'm sure I'm not the only one around here who hasn't read it." Tess opened the kitchen door. "Winnie, would you come here a minute, please?"

Their willowy cook, wiping her hands on her apron, appeared.

"Have you read *Uncle Tom's Cabin*?" Tess asked.

"Of course." Winne's eyes twinkled. "Everyone has." She pointed at the picture. "That's Eliza and Little Harry, crossing the Ohio River."

"Have you ever seen this picture before?" LuAnn asked her.

"Never." She pivoted and chuckled. "Now, I need to get back to my scones."

"Thank you," Tess said, "for proving me wrong..."

Winnie laughed as she started to waltz back into the kitchen.

"Wait," LuAnn asked. "Do you remember where you got the copy you read? Did the Marietta library have it?"

Winnie's eyes widened as she stopped in the doorway. "I'm sure they did. Probably more than one copy. But the one I read belonged to my parents. I think a lot of people, back then, had copies of the book. Of course, it was just a paperback. It probably cost fifty cents or so."

"You're probably right." LuAnn laughed. "Now it would probably be twenty times that for a paperback."

"Go check at Morrison's Books and let me know," Winnie teased as she stepped the rest of the way into the kitchen.

LuAnn laughed and turned back toward Tess. "I'll do that sometime soon, but in the meantime, I'm going to take this over to the museum to show Maybelline."

LuAnn wrapped the picture in a brand-new shower curtain, taping the sides up with packing tape. Then she put on her raincoat and braved the icy sideways rain that felt cold enough to turn into snow at any minute. She rushed to her car, turned on the engine and the heat, and then drove to the museum.

When she entered the museum, she called out, "Maybelline! You're never going to guess what I found!"

Maybelline, whose gray eyes seemed to signal fatigue, sat at a table with a man who appeared to be in his late fifties with a thinning head of gray hair. He wore a tweed jacket and blue jeans.

The man stood as LuAnn approached. "I'm Dale Sweet." He extended his hand. "From the Harriet Beecher Stowe Museum in Cincinnati."

She put the frame on the floor and held it steady with her left hand as she shook Dale's hand with her right. "LuAnn Sherrill, from Wayfarers Inn."

"Oh, I tried to get a reservation there." Dale's grip was firm. "But you were booked."

"We are." LuAnn smiled. Early March wasn't usually their busy time, so she was thrilled they were full. "Where are you staying instead?"

"Out at the Butterfly Farms and Bed-and-Breakfast."

"Oh, I bet Clint Lowery is taking good care of you."

Dale smiled. "He is." Then he pointed to the package. "What did you bring with you?"

LuAnn glanced at Maybelline. "Are you ready to see this?"

Maybelline nodded.

LuAnn placed the bottom of the frame on the table and began peeling back the packing tape. "I found this in the basement of the inn, tucked inside a crumbling wall."

As LuAnn pulled away the last of the plastic, Maybelline clapped her hands together, and LuAnn detected a moment of surprise on Dale's face.

But then he shook his head. "The frame is incredible, but that print is one of probably thousands. They're really a dime a dozen."

LuAnn held the frame with one hand and took a step away from the print so she could get a better look. "Are you sure?"

He nodded. "Positive. I'm an expert on *Uncle Tom's Cabin* memorabilia. I've seen this print over and over and over."

"In this good a shape?" It appeared nearly perfect to LuAnn.

"Definitely." He pointed to the frame. "This, however, is amazing. Any idea where it came from?"

LuAnn shook her head.

"I'm guessing England," he said. "Which makes sense. *Uncle Tom's Cabin* was a huge hit across the pond—over one million copies were sold there in just the first year, compared to 300,000 here in the US. It was the biggest best seller, after the Bible of course, of its time."

LuAnn was impressed by his knowledge.

"Sorry the print isn't worth anything." His bushy eyebrows shot up. "But that frame. Now that's another matter."

"How much do you think it's worth?"

"Oh, four, maybe five hundred dollars."

LuAnn's heart sank. He'd made it sound as if it was worth thousands. She turned toward Maybelline. "So, do you want the print for the exhibit?"

Maybelline's wrinkles grew more pronounced when she frowned. "Let me think about it.... I'm a little overwhelmed today. We've had lots of visitors, considering how stormy it is. And I've had special requests to look at all sorts of artifacts and no help on a day I could have really used it, with Dale here."

LuAnn nodded in sympathy.

Maybelline shrugged and glanced at Dale. "What do you think?"

He shook his head. "We have a couple of prints at the museum we can loan you. Ones printed here, in the US."

"All right then." LuAnn started rewrapping the print, disappointed that Maybelline didn't want the picture. "It's been nice to meet you, Dale. I hope you'll stay with us at the inn next time you're in town."

He chuckled. "I will, as long as you have room."

Back at the inn, LuAnn grabbed the step stool, a hammer, and a couple of nails and began hanging the print in the lobby, determined to have their own tribute to Harriet Beecher Stowe. As she did, a couple came through the front door. The man, who had a head full of sandy hair and a square chin, had a closed umbrella in his hand. Rain rolled off their luggage—three roller bags—as they paused for a moment, glancing around the lobby. Both wore black wool coats and fashionable leather shoes, and the woman wore a cobalt blue scarf around her neck. Everything about them appeared to be professional and put together.

"Welcome to Wayfarers Inn," LuAnn called out then turned her attention back to the print, checking its position. Satisfied, she climbed down from the stool. As she headed to the counter, she said, "I'll check you in over here."

The couple met her at the counter, and the man said with an English accent, "Ian and Anya Belknap."

LuAnn had noticed the name Anya on the guest list for the day. She'd had a student over twenty years ago with that name.

LuAnn found their names on the list again and then raised her head. She smiled at the woman, who had long dark hair and deep brown eyes, and her heart skipped a beat. "Anya?" The word came out as a gasp.

The woman smiled and then said, with a bit of an Eastern European accent, "Yes, it's me, Miss Sherrill." Anya didn't seem surprised at all to see LuAnn.

LuAnn placed her hand on her chest. "What are you doing here?"

Anya glanced toward her husband. "We were coming to Ohio for business, and when I found out you were part owner of this historic inn, I told Ian we had to stay here."

"But how did you know?"

"Oh, I was thinking through my past a few months ago, thinking about when I first came to the US, and I found you online."

LuAnn wasn't sure if that was a good thing or not. Anya was one of the most difficult students she'd ever had, much to her own shame. Looking back, she'd been too hard on the girl. Anya was a Bosnian refugee, and as much as LuAnn tried to reach her—and push her—she never felt she succeeded. And she doubted Anya had fond memories from her high school years.

In fact, looking back, LuAnn realized Anya had reason to resent her. She didn't say any of that, of course. Instead she said, "Well, it's wonderful to see you and have you here as a guest." Then she launched into her usual welcome speech.

Anya listened, but her husband started looking around the lobby again. His eyes fell on the print.

As LuAnn finished her welcome, Ian said, "Tell me about the *Uncle Tom's Cabin* picture."

"I just found it in the basement today, but I've already been told it's quite common."

He stepped closer. "Oh, I doubt that."

"Ian specializes in nineteenth-century art," Anya explained.

"Mostly American," he said. "But occasionally from England too," he said. "Which is where this print originated."

"Yes," LuAnn said, "that's what I've been told."

"Harriet Beecher Stowe, along with her husband, visited Great Britain in 1853," Ian explained. "She was greeted with warm enthusiasm everywhere she went, from the wharf where her ship from the United States docked to royalty to the people who gathered around her carriage wherever she went. When she visited Glasgow, over two thousand people gathered to sing hymns and welcome Harriet with stomping and clapping and shouting."

His words sent shivers down LuAnn's spine. She remembered reading about the trip at one time, but she reveled in hearing about it from the perspective of an Englishman.

"Forgive me," Ian said. "I'm afraid I could go on and on about Harriet Beecher Stowe."

"Please do," LuAnn said. "I'm a big fan of hers too." And it was a treat to have a history lesson given with an English accent. "But I'm afraid the picture isn't anything special. I've been told the prints are a dime a dozen."

Ian shook his head. "I don't believe that's true." He pulled a camera from the leather bag hanging on his shoulder. "Mind if I take a photo?"

"Of course not," LuAnn said as another guest came through the front door, a backpack slung over his right shoulder and a pair of dress clothes hanging from his left hand. He was coughing. LuAnn hoped he wasn't ill.

She grabbed two keys for the honeymoon suite for Anya. There was no note on the registration that it was, in fact, their honeymoon. Perhaps they simply wanted the largest room.

The new arrival stopped at the picture too as Ian asked LuAnn, "What do you know about the print?"

"Nothing, really," she answered. "I found it in the basement today, tucked back in a wall. It had been wrapped with care and survived the years intact."

Ian ran his finger along the frame. "Someone took care of it right and proper. We don't see that sort of attention very often to items tucked away in basements." He tucked his camera back into his bag. "I'll put more thought into this and let you know what it might be worth."

As LuAnn gave Anya directions to the honeymoon suite, Ian and the other man spoke with each other. A couple of times the man turned his head away and coughed.

"I hope we'll have a chance to catch up while you're here," LuAnn said to Anya. "I'd love to hear how the last twenty years have treated you."

"I'd like that." Anya's expression was serious, without a trace of a smile. Then she turned to her husband. "I have the keys. Let's go on up."

As they headed toward the elevator, the man with the backpack approached the counter. "Bryson Cast..." He coughed again, but this time he couldn't seem to stop.

"Are you all right?" LuAnn asked.

The man nodded as he reached into his backpack, pulled out an inhaler, and used it. He continued to cough and used the inhaler again.

"Can I get you a drink of water?" LuAnn asked.

He shook his head and pulled out his phone and managed to say, "I think I need a breathing treatment, is all. I'll head up to the hospital. Could I leave my hang-up clothes here?"

"Of course." LuAnn took the clothes, hung them in the office, and then quickly checked Bryson in and gave him a key. "Hopefully we'll see you soon—but if it's late, let yourself in. Just make sure the front door is closed and locked behind you."

He nodded, took the key, and then turned to leave.

LuAnn walked to the door with him. "Please let us know if you need anything."

Bryson waved and coughed again as he stepped out the door.

LuAnn shivered—she'd never checked a guest in and then sent him off to the hospital.

A half hour later, Marco and Sallie Gomez arrived with their seven-month-old baby. LuAnn had set up a crib in

Moonlight and Snowflakes earlier in the day for the little one and had been looking forward to meeting them. She knew, from when he made the reservation, that Marco worked at a small college out West and was attending a leadership conference at Marietta College.

As she greeted them warmly, the baby began to cry. "She's exhausted," Sallie said. "It's been a long day." The little one was dressed in a purple down jacket, a pair of leggings, and a miniature pair of sheepskin boots. Her dark hair was thick and pulled back in a bow. She rubbed her face against her mother's shoulder, muffling her crying.

"Did you travel all the way today?" LuAnn asked.

Marco shook his head. "Sallie's parents live in Ashland. We arrived there a couple of days ago and then drove down today."

"Well, welcome to Marietta and to Wayfarers Inn. We're so happy you've chosen to stay here."

"I hope Lucy won't be too disruptive," Sallie said.

"She won't be," LuAnn responded. "We've had plenty of babies as guests. She'll do fine."

As the couple headed toward the elevator, LuAnn hoped Lucy would be fine. She'd put them on the third floor, where she hoped the baby's crying would be less likely to be heard by others.

The afternoon and evening progressed along. A few times, LuAnn wondered how Bryson was doing. Thankfully he called just before she was ready to go up to bed. "They're going to have me spend the night," he said. "I'll see you in the morning." At the moment, he seemed to be breathing all right.

Relieved he was getting good care, LuAnn went to bed, hoping the next day would be less eventful.

Sometime during the night the electricity went out, most likely due to the storm, because when LuAnn woke in the morning her alarm clock flickered and was behind thirty-four minutes. She quickly reset it and then got ready for the day.

A half hour later, as she padded through the lobby on the way to start the coffee in the kitchen, she stopped. Something was wrong. Her eyes darted around the walls. The print was missing.

She sent a text to Tess and Janice. *Did one of you put Eliza somewhere else?*

They responded. *No* and *No* and then Tess texted, *We're on our way down.*

As Janice made the coffee, LuAnn checked the front door and the back door. Both were secure. Then she and Tess searched the sitting area, the dining room, the basement, and the landings of each floor. Perhaps someone was playing a trick on them. When they returned empty-handed to the kitchen, to the smell of coffee brewing and scones baking, Winnie and Janice were putting the breakfast items on the buffet table for the guests.

"Who would have taken the print?" Janice asked.

"Ian Belknap was interested in it," LuAnn said. "I suppose I'll need to ask him if he knows anything about it going missing." Which would give Anya even more reason to dislike her.

Thankfully she didn't have to ask Ian. As soon as he and Anya came down for breakfast, he approached her. "Excuse me, Miss Sherrill—"

"LuAnn," she said, smiling at him and then Anya.

"LuAnn," Ian said in his lovely British accent. "Why did you take the print down?"

"I didn't," she said. "It's gone missing."

His eyes narrowed. "Someone stole it?"

LuAnn shrugged. "We're not sure, but it appears that could be a possibility."

Seemingly stunned, he said, "What an unfortunate business." He sighed. "Perhaps someone else realized its value too. I should have suggested you have it appraised before you decided to leave it hanging out in the open like that, but from what I found last night, it's worth at least five thousand dollars. Not a fortune by any means, but more than 'a dime a dozen.'"

LuAnn wasn't sure whether to believe him or not. He was convincing—but then again, so was Dale Sweet.

A half hour later, as Ian and Anya ventured out the door to walk around Marietta, the phone rang.

"I'll get it," LuAnn said, hoping for an update from Bryson Cast.

That would have to wait. A hysterical Maybelline was on the line. "The museum has been broken into," she wailed.

"Oh, no." LuAnn's heart began to race. "Was anything taken?"

"Only one item—well, two—as far as I can tell."

"What were they?"

"Both volumes of *Uncle Tom's Cabin*."